STUDENT ACTIVITIES MANUAL

for

ADLER AND PROCTOR'S

LOOKING OUT/LOOKING IN

TWELFTH EDITION

JEANNE ELMHORST
Central New Mexico Community College

THOMSON
WADSWORTH

Australia · Brazil · Canada · Mexico · Singapore · Spain · United Kingdom · United States

THOMSON

™

WADSWORTH

Student Activities Manual for Looking Out, Looking In
Twelfth Edition
Ronald B. Adler · Russell F. Proctor II

Thomson Higher Education
25 Thomson Place
Boston, MA 02210-1202
USA

For more information about our products, contact us at:
Thomson Learning Academic Resource Center
1-800-423-0563

For permission to use material from this text or product, submit a request online at **http://www.thomsonrights.com**

Any additional questions about permissions can be submitted by e-mail to **thomsonrights@thomson.com**

Printed in Canada
1 2 3 4 5 09 08 07 06

ISBN-13: 978-0-495-10129-1
ISBN-10: 0-495-10129-X

CONTENTS

CHAPTER 3   PERCEPTION: WHAT YOU SEE IS WHAT YOU GET

CHAPTER 4   EMOTIONS: THINKING, FEELING AND COMMUNICATING

CHAPTER 9   COMMUNICATION AND RELATIONAL DYNAMICS

CHAPTER 10   IMPROVING COMMUNICATION CLIMATES

PREFACE

Welcome to the *Student Activities Manual* for *Looking Out/Looking In*, Twelfth Edition. This *Student Activities Manual* is designed to enhance student learning. The *Student Activities Manual* contains more than 50 exercises and more than 500 study test items designed to build understanding of principles and proficiency in skills introduced in the text.

Chapters in the *Student Activities Manual* parallel the chapters in *Looking Out/Looking In*. The following areas in each chapter combine to provide a thorough, student-centered learning package:

•**Outlines.** Extended outlines of each chapter begin each section. Many instructors ask students to use the outlines as a lecture guide in class or a place to take notes as they read the chapter.

•**Activities.** Students who complete the activities in this workbook can develop understanding and skill in each area through a choice of exercises.

Skill Builder activities — designed primarily to help students identify the target behavior in a number of common interpersonal communication situations.

Invitation to Insight activities — designed to help students discover how newly learned principles can be applied in their everyday lives. They can be grouped together to form a "Communication Journal" for the entire course. While these activities are usually designed for individual use, they can provide the structure for small group discussion or lecture/discussion.

Oral Skill activities — designed to allow students to actually exhibit communication behaviors they have studied. They are designed for individual, dyadic, or small group use in a classroom or lab setting.

Mediated Communication activities — designed to challenge students to apply interpersonal communication principles to the many mediated contexts they encounter. They are designed for individual, dyadic, or small group use in a classroom or lab setting.

Your Call activities — designed to prompt analysis and ethical choices among students. They are designed primarily for group discussion in a classroom or lab setting.

Group Discussion and Group Activities — designed to encourage collaborative learning, listening skills, affective and cognitive development, and cognitive complexity.

Student observations in many exercises will lead to class discussions on how to apply the newly learned principles in the "real world" of one's interpersonal relationships. Exercises help students to move beyond simply understanding the principles of interpersonal communication and actually to perform more effectively in a variety of communication situations.

•**Study Guide.** Crossword Puzzle, Matching, True/False, Completion, and Multiple Choice items review and reinforce for students as they work at their own pace. Answer keys for all the study guide activities are found at the end of each chapter.

The *Student Activities Manual* can help develop more effective communication, both in class and in students' lives outside the classroom.

C H A P T E R   O N E

A First Look at Interpersonal Communication

OUTLINE

Use this outline to take notes as you read the chapter in the text and/or as your instructor lectures in class.

I. **INTRODUCTION TO INTERPERSONAL COMMUNICATION**
   A. **Communication Is Important**
   B. **We Communicate to Satisfy Needs**
      1. Physical needs
      2. Identity needs
      3. Social needs
         a. Pleasure
         b. Affection
         c. Companionship
         d. Escape
         e. Relaxation
         f. Control
      4. Practical goals
         a. Instrumental goals
            1) Influence other's behavior
            2) Career success
         b. Maslow's basic needs
            1) Physical
            2) Safety
            3) Social
            4) Self-esteem
            5) Self-actualization

II. **THE PROCESS OF COMMUNICATION**
   A. **Linear View**
      1. Sender
      2. Encodes
      3. Message
      4. Channel
      5. Receiver
      6. Decodes
      7. Noise - external
   B. **Transactional View**
      1. Communicator is simultaneously sender and receiver

1. Environments
   a. physical
   b. cultural
   c. experiential

2. Noise disrupts communication
   a. External
   b. Physiological
   c. Psychological

3. Transactional communication is *with* others

4. Definition

III. COMMUNICATION PRINCIPLES AND MISCONCEPTIONS
A. Communication Principles
1. Communication can be intentional or unintentional
2. It's impossible not to communicate
3. Communication is irreversible
4. Communication is unrepeatable
5. Communication has content and relational dimensions.

B. Communication Misconceptions
1. Meanings are not in words
2. Successful communication doesn't always involve shared understanding
3. More communication is not always better
4. No single person or event causes another's reaction
5. Communication will not solve all problems

IV. THE NATURE OF INTERPERSONAL COMMUNICATION
A. Two Views of Interpersonal Communication
1. Quantitative --dyadic (two people involved)
2. Qualitative view emphasizes
   a. Uniqueness – rules and roles
   b. Irreplaceability
   c. Interdependence
   d. Disclosure
   e. Intrinsic rewards
   f. Scarcity

B. Technology and Interpersonal Communication
1. CMC (computer mediated communication) can enrich communication
2. CMC can increase the quantity and quality of interpersonal communication
3. CMC can enhance, not replace face-to-face communication

C. Personal and Impersonal Communication: A Matter of Balance

V. WHAT MAKES AN EFFECTIVE COMMUNICATOR?
A. Communication Competence Defined
1. No ideal way exists
2. Situational

   3. Relational
   4. Can be learned
   B. Characteristics of Competent Communicators
      1. Wide range of behaviors
      2. Ability to choose most appropriate behavior
         a. Context
         b. Goal
         c. Knowledge of the other person
      3. Skill at performing behaviors
         a. Beginning awareness
         b. Awkwardness
         c. Skillfulness
         d. Integration
      4. Cognitive complexity
      5. Empathy
      6. Self-monitoring
      7. Commitment
         a. Commitment to the other person
         b. Commitment to the message
   C. Competence is Intercultural
      1. Co-cultures include nationality, age, race/ethnicity, occupation, sexual orientation, ability, religion, activity
      2. Learn specific cultural rules
      3. Develop motivation, tolerance for ambiguity, open-mindedness, knowledge and skill.

KEY TERMS

channel

co-culture

cognitive complexity

communication

communication competence

computer-mediated communication (CMC)

decoding

dyad

encoding

environment

immediacy

impersonal communication

instrumental goals

interpersonal communication (quantitative and qualitative)

linear communication model

message

noise (external, physiological, psychological)

receiver

self-monitoring

sender

transactional communication model

ACTIVITIES

1.1 COMMUNICATION SKILLS INVENTORY

Activity Type: Invitation to Insight

PURPOSES

1. To discover how satisfied you are with the way you communicate in various situations.
2. To preview some topics that will be covered in *Looking Out/Looking In*.

INSTRUCTIONS

1. Below you will find several communication-related situations. As you read each item, imagine yourself in that situation.
2. For each instance, answer the following question: *How satisfied am I with the way I would communicate in this situation and ones like it?* You can express your answers by placing one of the following numbers in the space by each item:

5 = Completely satisfied with my probable action
4 = Generally, though not totally, satisfied with my probable action
3 = About equally satisfied and dissatisfied with my probable action
2 = Generally, though not totally, dissatisfied with my probable action
1 = Totally dissatisfied with my probable action

_____ 1. A new acquaintance has just shared some personal experiences with you that make you think you'd like to develop a closer relationship. You have experienced the same things and are now deciding whether to reveal these personal experiences. (8, 9)

_____ 2. You've become involved in a political discussion with someone whose views are the complete opposite of yours. The other person asks, "Can't you at least understand why I feel as I do?" (3, 7)

_____ 3. You are considered a responsible adult by virtually everyone except one relative who still wants to help you make all your decisions. You value your relationship with this person, but you want to be seen as more independent. (10, 11)

_____ 4. In a mood of self-improvement a friend asks you to describe the one or two ways you think he or she could behave better. You're willing to do so, but need to express yourself in a clear and helpful way. (3, 5, 10)

_____ 5. A close companion tells you that you've been behaving "differently" lately and asks if you know what he or she means. (5, 6, 7)

_____ 6. You've grown to appreciate a new friend a great deal lately, and you want to express your feelings to this friend. (4)

_____ 7. An amateur writer you know has just shown you his or her latest batch of poems and asked your opinion of them. You don't think they are very good. It's time for your reply. (5, 10)

_____ 8. You've found certain behaviors of an important person in your life have become more and more bothersome to you. It's getting harder to keep your feelings to yourself. (4, 10)

_____ 9. You're invited to a party at which everyone except the host will be a stranger to you. Upon hearing about this, a friend says, "Gee, if I were going I'd feel like an outsider. They probably won't have much to do with you." How do you feel? (2)

_____ 10. A friend comes to you feeling very upset about a recent incident and asks for advice. You suspect that there is more to the problem than just this one incident. You really want to help the friend. (7)

_____ 11. You find yourself defending the behavior of a friend against the criticisms of a third person. The critic accuses you of seeing only what you want to see and ignoring the rest. (2, 4, 5, 10)

_____ 12. A boss or instructor asks you to explain a recent assignment to a companion who has been absent. You are cautioned to explain the work clearly so there will be no misunderstandings. (5)

_____ 13. You ask an acquaintance for help with a problem. She says yes, but the way the message is expressed leaves you thinking she'd rather not. You do need the help, but only if it's sincerely offered. (3, 6, 10)

_____ 14. A roommate always seems to be too busy to do the dishes when it's his or her turn, and you've wound up doing them most of the time. You resent the unequal sharing of responsibility and want to do something about it. (11)

_____ 15. A new acquaintance has become quite interested in getting to know you better, but you feel no interest yourself. You've heard that this person is extremely sensitive and insecure. (1, 2)

You can use the results of this survey in two ways. By looking at each question you can see how satisfied you are with your behavior in that specific type of situation. A response of 1 or 2 on any single question is an obvious signal that you can profit from working on that situation. Parenthetical numbers following each item indicate the chapters of *Looking Out/Looking In* which focus on that subject.

By totaling your score for all of the items you can get an idea of how satisfied you are with your overall ability to communicate in interpersonal situations. A score of 68–75 suggests high satisfaction, 58–67 indicates moderate satisfaction, while 45–57 shows that you feel dissatisfied with your communication behavior nearly half the time.

Another valuable way to use this activity is to make a second inventory at the end of the course. Have you improved? Are there still areas you will need to work on?

1.2 EXPANDING YOUR COMMUNICATION EFFECTIVENESS

Activity Type: Invitation to Insight

PURPOSES

1. To broaden your repertoire of effective communication behaviors and your skill at performing them.
2. To identify the most appropriate communication behaviors in important situations.

INSTRUCTIONS

1. Use the space below to identify three areas in which you would like to communicate more effectively. (e.g., I can't take "no" well. I have trouble telling people what I don't like. People take my intentions wrong.)
2. For each area, identify a person you have observed who communicates effectively in this situation. Describe this person's communication behavior.
3. Describe how you could adapt these behaviors to your own life.

EXAMPLE

a. Area in which you would like to communicate more effectively
    Making conversation with people I've just met.
b. Model who communicates effectively in this area *My friend Rich*
c. Model's behavior *He asks sincere questions of people he's just met, compliments them enthusiastically, and smiles a lot.*
d. How could you apply these behaviors? *I can spend more time thinking about people I've just met and less time thinking self-consciously about my own nervousness. Then I can focus on parts of these new people that interest me and let the other person know I'm interested. The key seems to be sincerity: I have to really mean what I say and not use questions and compliments as tricks.*

SITUATION 1

a. Area in which you would like to communicate more effectively

    _____

b. Model who communicates effectively in this area _____

c. Model's behavior _____

    _____

d. How could you apply these behaviors? _____

    _____

    _____

SITUATION 2

a. Area in which you would like to communicate more effectively

_____

b. Model who communicates effectively in this area _____

c. Model's behavior _____

_____

d. How could you apply these behaviors? _____

_____

_____

_____

SITUATION 3

a. Area in which you would like to communicate more effectively

_____

b. Model who communicates effectively in this area _____

c. Model's behavior _____

_____

d. How could you apply these behaviors? _____

_____

_____

_____

SUMMARY REFLECTION

a. What comparisons or contrasts can you identify in the three situations?

_____

b. How can you use this exercise to guide your study of communication? _____

_____

_____

1.3 CMC-COMPUTER MEDIATED COMMUNICATION
ACTIVITY TYPE: INVITATION TO INSIGHT/GROUP DISCUSSION

PURPOSE

To evaluate the face-to-face and mediated channels you use to communicate interpersonally.

INSTRUCTIONS

Answer the questions below. Then, in small or large group discussion compare your experiences with classmates.

1. List all the mediated channels you use to communicate interpersonally.

    _____

    _____

2. Describe the reasons you use mediated channels. Consider both *practical* reasons (e.g., to communicate over distance) and *strategic* ones (e.g., to avoid face-to-face confrontation).

    _____

    _____

    _____

3. Describe situations in which your communication is more effective using mediated channels and explain why.

    _____

    _____

4. Describe situations in which your communication is less effective using mediated channels and explain why.

    _____

    _____

5. How do you think relationships are affected when they **begin** through mediated communication rather than face-to-face? Is this different if the relationship is professional or personal?

    _____

6. What are the differences in the quantity, frequency and quality of mediated communication you experience with different generations (parents, grandparents)? Do you use CMC more frequently with certain age-groups? Why or why not?

_____

_____

_____

7. Your text cites a study that states that CMC encourages greater offline interaction with close friends. What is your experience? If you e-mail more, do you also see each other more?

_____

_____

8. Do you prefer CMC over face-to-face to meet some needs for information? Do you prefer e-mail, phone, text-messaging, or face-to-face communication with instructors, family, friends, co-workers, supervisors? Does this vary with the person's age, gender, role? How do you let others know your preferences?

_____

_____

1.4 YOUR CALL – COMMUNICATION BASICS
Activity Type: Skill Builder/Group Discussion

PURPOSES

1. To reflect upon and judge a communication transaction in terms of the needs of the persons involved.
2. To highlight communication principles and misconceptions that may be present.
3. To use the communication model to identify potential communication problems and recommend solutions.

INSTRUCTIONS

Use the case below and the discussion questions that follow to discuss the variety of communication issues involved in effective communication. Make notes on this page, add other pages on your own, or prepare a group report/analysis based on your discussion. Add your own experiences to individualize the analysis to make it **Your Call**.

CASE

Lucia and Caleb have been dating one another exclusively for four months. They both have part-time jobs and hope to complete their college studies within two years. Caleb thinks they should move in together. Lucia is reluctant to agree until she has more commitment from Caleb. Caleb doesn't want to make promises he can't keep. Lucia thinks that if they just communicate more they will be able to solve the problem, but Caleb thinks that talking about it more won't help.

1. What needs (physical, identity, social, and/or practical) do Lucia and Caleb seem to have?

_____

_____

2. Identify one element of the communication model that might help explain some of the communication problems they are having and help them communicate more effectively.

_____

_____

3. What communication principles and/or misconceptions described in Chapter 1 may be operating in this situation?

_____

_____

1.5 ANALYZING AND APPLYING

Activity Type: Invitation to Insight

PURPOSES

1. To analyze a communication situation using communication concepts.
2. To apply communication concepts to better understand and improve communication.

INSTRUCTIONS

Answer the questions below by reflecting on a communication situation.

Think of a situation in which you thought your communication was ineffective and/or you were dissatisfied with your communication. Briefly describe the situation and what created dissatisfaction for you.

_____

_____

1. What channels did you use to communicate? What other channels might have been more effective? Why? _____

_____

2. What types of noise (external, physiological, psychological) were present for you? For the other person? How could you have eliminated or minimized some of the noise?

_____

_____

_____

_____

3. Think about the context (time and place). Was it a good time and a good place? If so, why? Could you have changed the time and place to improve communication? What context might have been better? Why?

_____

_____

_____

_____

4. Think about other elements (sender, receiver, messages, environments, encoding, decoding) in the communication process that you might have changed to create greater effectiveness and satisfaction. _____

_____

_____

_____

5.   Consider the Communication Misconceptions identified in your text :
      1.   *Meanings are not in words*
      2.   *Successful communication doesn't always involve shared understanding*
      3.   *More communication is not always better*
      4.   *No single person or event causes another's reaction*
      5.   *Communication will not solve all problems*
      Were any of the misconceptions contributing to ineffectiveness or dissatisfaction ? Explain
      how.

      _____

      _____

      _____

STUDY GUIDE

CHECK YOUR UNDERSTANDING

Across

1. two individuals communicating
2. the communication ability to accomplish one's relationship on terms that are acceptable to all parties
3. the social need to influence others
6. behavior that treats others as objects rather than individuals
8. the process of putting thoughts into symbols, most commonly words
9. information sent from one person to another
11. any force that interferes with effective communication
13. the dimension of a message that makes statements about how the parties feel toward one another

Down

1. the process during which a receiver attaches meaning to a message
2. the medium through which a messages passes from sender to receiver
4. communication in which the parties consider one another as unique individuals rather than objects

5. the field of experiences that leads a person to make sense of another's behavior
7. one who notices and attends to a message

10. One characteristic of a competent communicator is the ability to ____-monitor.
12. the creator of a message

TRUE/FALSE

Mark the statements below as true or false. Correct false statements on the lines below to create a true statement.

_____ 1. Studies show your physical health may be affected by communication.

_____

_____ 2. We learn who we are through communication with others and their reactions to us.

_____

_____ 3. Communication skills are usually much less important in getting a job than technical competence, work experience, or a degree.

_____

_____ 4. Instrumental goals are the same thing as social needs.

_____

_____ 5. Psychologist Abraham Maslow claims that basic needs must be satisfied before people concern themselves with higher order needs.

_____

_____ 6. The linear view of communication suggests that communication flows in one direction, from sender to receiver.

_____

_____ 7. The transactional model of communication shows that communication is something we do *to* others.

_____

_____ 8. We can decide not to communicate in many ways, such as leaving the room.

_____

_____ 9. Luckily, communication will always help us solve our problems.

_____

_____ 10. Dyadic communication is the earliest form of interaction we experience and the most common type of communication.

_____

_____ 11. What qualifies as competent behavior in one culture might be completely inept, or even offensive, in another.

_____

_____ 12. In order to build a competent relationship, we need to get rid of our need to maintain some space between ourselves and the other person.

_____

_____ 13. You can build competent relationships only if you put the other person's needs ahead of yours.

_____

_____ 14. Effective communicators are able to choose their actions from a wide range of behaviors.

_____

_____ 15. Most relationships can be classified as purely interpersonal or purely impersonal.

_____

COMPLETION

Fill in the blanks below with the correct terms chosen from the list below.

instrumental goals	social needs	identity needs	physiological noise
psychological noise	self-monitoring	co-cultures	commitment
cognitive complexity	empathy		

1. _____ are the needs we have to define who we are.

2. _____ are the needs we have to link ourselves with others.

3. _____ are the needs we have to get others to behave in ways we want.

4. _____ refers to the forces within a communicator that interfere with the ability to express or understand a message accurately.

5. _____ refers to the biological factors in the receiver or sender that interfere with accurate reception of messages.

6. _____ groups that shape our perceptions: ethnic, national, religious

7. _____ is the desire to interact and continue the relationship.

8. _____ is the ability to construct a variety of different frameworks for viewing an issue.

9. _____ is the process of paying close attention to your behavior in order to shape the way you behave.

10. _____ is the ability to imagine how an issue might look from the other's point of view.

MULTIPLE CHOICE

Choose the letter of the communication process element that is most illustrated by the description found below. Italicized words provide clues.
  a. encode
  b. decode
  c. channel
  d. message/feedback
  e. noise (external, physiological or psychological)
  f. environment

_____ 1. The children make a *videotape* of themselves to send to their grandparents instead of writing a *letter*.

_____ 2. Marjorie tries to *decide the best way* to tell Martin that she can't go to Hawaii with him.

_____ 3. Martin *decides* Marjorie means she doesn't love him when she says she can't go to Hawaii.

_____ 4. It's so *hot* in the room that Brad has a hard time concentrating on what his partner is telling him.

_____ 5. Linda *smiles* while Larry is talking to her.

_____ 6. Brooke is *daydreaming* about her date while Allison is talking to her.

_____ 7. Since Jacob *has never been married*, it's difficult for him to understand why his *married* friend Brent wants to spend less time with him.

_____ 8. Whitney says, *"I'm positive about my vote."*

_____ 9. Richard *thinks* Jon wants to leave when he waves to him.

_____ 10. Laura *winks* when she *says* she's serious and *gestures* with her arms.

_____ 11. Erin is from a *wealthy* family and Kate from a *poor* one. They have a serious conflict about how to budget their money.

_____ 12. Jack has been feeling a *cold* coming on all day while he has sat through the meeting.

Choose the *best* answer for each of the questions below:

13. The concept of co-cultures is closest to the concept of differing
    a. environments
    b. relational messages
    c. self-monitoring
    d. impersonal communication

14. Martin Buber's concept of communication that is truly interpersonal is called
    a. I-You
    b. I-They
    c. I-It
    d. I-We

15. Improving intercultural compentence involves all of the following except
    a. motivation
    b. open-mindedness
    c. knowledge and skill
    d. avoiding ambiguity

16. According to the quantitative definition of interpersonal communication, interpersonal communication occurs when
    a. two people interact with one another, usually face to face.
    b. you watch a TV show about relationships.
    c. you read a romance novel.
    d. large numbers of people communicate

17. All of the following statements are true <u>except</u>
    a. Communication has content and relational dimensions.
    b. Communication is irreversible.
    c. Communication can be unintentional.
    d. Communication is repeatable.

18. All of the following statements are true <u>except</u>
    a. Meanings are not in words.
    b. More communication is not always better.
    c. Communication can solve all your problems.
    d. Communication is not a natural ability.

19. According to most studies cited in your text, CMC
    a. diminishes the amount of face-to-face interaction
    b. enriches and promotes more social interaction
    c. leads to more impersonal communication in families
    d. makes people more aware of gender and age differences

20. When you are able to perform communication skills without thinking about how you should behave, you have entered the skill stage of
    a. awareness.
    b. awkwardness.
    c. skillfulness.
    d. integration.

CHAPTER 1 STUDY GUIDE ANSWERS

CROSSWORD PUZZLE

A crossword grid with the following filled answers:

- Across 2: competence
- Across 3: comtrol
- Across 6: impersonal
- Across 8: encoding
- Across 9: message
- Across 11: noise
- Across 13: relational
- Down 1: dvad
- Down: chann(l)
- Down: control/od...
- Down 5: environment
- Down: message...

(Letters visible in grid: d v a d / competence / h / comtrol / a / n / o / n / e(5) i(6) impersonal / i(4) / encoding / n / g / e / t / l / v / c / e / i / r / r / e / o / i / p / v / e / n o i s e / e / r / m / e(12) e / r / m e s s a g e / n / s / e / n / o / l / d / n / t / relational / l / f / r / l)

TRUE/FALSE

1. T	4. F	7. F	10. T
2. T	5. T	8. F	11. T
3. F	6. T	9. F	12. F

COMPLETION

1. identity needs
2. social needs
3. instrumental goals
4. psychological noise
5. physiological noise
6. co-cultures
7. commitment
8. cognitive complexity
9. self-monitoring
10. empathy

MULTIPLE CHOICE

1. c	5. d	9. b	13. a	17. d
2. a	6. e	10. c	14. a	18. c
3. b	7. f	11. f	15. d	19. b
4. e	8. d	12. e	16. a	20. d

CHAPTER TWO

Communication and Identity:
Creating and Presenting the Self

OUTLINE

Use this outline to take notes as you read the chapter in the text and/or as your instructor lectures in class.

I. **COMMUNICATION AND THE SELF-CONCEPT**
   A. **Definitions**
      1. Self-concept: The relatively stable set of perceptions you hold of yourself
      2. Self-esteem: Evaluation of your self-worth
   B. **Biological and Social Roots of the Self**
      1. Biology and the self
         a. Personality – characteristic ways of thinking and behaving
         b. Traits – a matter of degree
      2. Socialization and the self-concept
         a. Reflected appraisal (through significant others)
         b. Social comparison (through reference groups)
            1) superior/inferior
            2) same/different

   C. **Characteristics of the Self-Concept**
      1. The self-concept is subjective
         a. Obsolete information
         b. Distorted feedback
         c. Emphasis on perfection
         d. Social expectations
      2. The self-concept resists change (cognitive conservatism)
         a. Failure to acknowledge change
         b. Self-delusion and lack of growth
         c. Defensiveness
   D. **Culture, Gender and Identity**
      1. Culture
         a. Individualistic
         b. Collectivistic
      2. Sex and gender
   E. **The Self-Fulfilling Prophecy and Communication**
      1. Definition: expectations and behaviors based on expectations make an outcome more likely. (Four stages to the process)
      2. Types
         a. Self-imposed
         b. Imposed by others

F. **Changing Your Self-Concept**
    1. Have a realistic perception of yourself
    2. Have realistic expectations
    3. Have the will to change
    4. Have the skill to change

II. **PRESENTING THE SELF: COMMUNICATION AS IMPRESSION MANAGEMENT**

    A. **Public and Private Selves**
        1. Perceived self
        2. Presenting self (face)

    B. **Characteristics of Identity Management**
        1. We strive to construct multiple identities.
        3.   Identity management is collaborative.
        4. Identity management can be deliberate or unconscious.
        4. Identity management varies by situation.
        5. People differ in their degree of identity management.
           (high and low self-monitors)

    C. **Why Manage Identities?**
        1.   To start and manage relationships
        2.   To gain compliance of others
        3.   To save others' face

    D. **How Do We Manage Identities?**
        1. Face-to-face impression management
           a. Manner
               1) Words
               2) Nonverbal behavior
           b. Appearance
           c. Setting
        2. Impression management in mediated communication

    E. **Impression Management and Honesty**

KEY TERMS

cognitive conservatism

face

identity management

perceived self

personality

presenting self

reference groups

reflected appraisal

self-concept

self-esteem

self-fulfilling prophecy

significant others

social comparison

ACTIVITIES

2.1 WHO DO YOU THINK YOU ARE?

Activity Type: Invitation to Insight

PURPOSE

To identify the biological and social aspects of your self-concept.

INSTRUCTIONS

1. First, if possible, take an The Jung Typology Test at http://www.humanmetrics.com/cgi-win/JTypes2.asp. This will get you thinking about the way you describe yourself.
2. For each category below, supply the words or phrases that describe you best.
3. After filling in the spaces within each category, organize your responses so that the most fundamental characteristic is listed first, with the rest of the items following in order of descending importance.

PART A: IDENTIFY THE ELEMENTS OF YOUR SELF-CONCEPT

1. How would you describe your social behaviors (friendly, shy, aloof, talkative, etc.)?

   a. _____   b. _____   c. _____

2. How would you describe your personality traits (stable, extraverted, introverted, etc.)?

   a. _____   b. _____   c. _____

3. What beliefs do you hold strongly (vegetarian, green, Christian, pacifist, etc.)?

   a. _____   b. _____   c. _____

4. What social roles are the most important in your life (brother, student, friend, bank teller, club president, etc.)?

   a. _____   b. _____   c. _____

5. How would you describe your intellectual capacity (curious, poor reader, good mathematician, etc.)?

   a. _____   b. _____   c. _____

6. How would you describe your physical condition and/or your appearance (fit, sedentary, tall, attractive, etc.)?

   a. _____   b. _____   c. _____

7. What talents do you possess or lack (good artist, lousy carpenter, competent swimmer, etc.)?

   a. _____   b. _____   c. _____

8. What other descriptors are important to describe you (cultural, ethnic, gender, sexual-orientation, moods, feelings, others)

   a. _____   b. _____   c. _____

Class _____   Name_____

PART B: ARRANGE YOUR SELF-CONCEPT ELEMENTS IN ORDER OF IMPORTANCE

1. _____   13. _____

2. _____   14. _____

3. _____   15. _____

4. _____   16. _____

5. _____   17. _____

6. _____   18. _____

7. _____   19. _____

8. _____   20. _____

9. _____   21. _____

10. _____   22. _____

11. _____   23. _____

12. _____   24. _____

Describe any factors that have contributed in a positive or negative way to the formation of your perceived self. Explain if some were due to obsolete information, social expectations, distorted feedback, or perfection beliefs. Include any other factors involved in the formation of your perceived self (for example, certain significant others, any strong reference groups).

_____

_____

_____

_____

What significant others or reference groups contributed to your self-concept? How?

_____

_____

NOTE: You will use these descriptors in Activity 2.2.

2.2 SELF-CONCEPT INVENTORY
Activity Type: Invitation to Insight

PURPOSE

1. To give you a clearer picture of how you see yourself (your perceived self).
2. To illustrate how others perceive you (presenting selves).

Note: Refer to Table 2.1 in your text for a list of self-selected adjectives that describe the perceived and presenting selves of college students.

INSTRUCTIONS

1. Transfer the list of up to 24 elements of your self-concept from the previous exercise (2.1) to index cards (or strips of paper).
2. Arrange your cards in a stack, with the one that *best* describes you at the top and the one that *least* describes you at the bottom.
3. Record the order in which you arranged the cards (1 is the most like you) in the Perceived Self column (Column 1). You may leave out some cards or add on to your list.
4. Without revealing your Perceived Self column, ask two other people (a friend, co-worker, roommate, family member, classmate) to arrange the descriptors in an order in which they see you. Record these perceptions in Columns 2 and 3. Neither should see Column 1 or the other person's column. Record the name/relationship of your reviewers at the top of the appropriate column.
5. Compare the three tables, circling any descriptors that are exactly the same across the three columns. Highlight any that have similar ranks (no more than three numbers different).
6. Answer the questions at the end of this exercise.

Column 1 Perceived Self	Column 2 Presenting Self to _____ (relationship to you)	Column 3 Presenting Self to _____ (relationship to you)
1. _____	1. _____	1. _____
2. _____	2. _____	2. _____
3. _____	3. _____	3. _____
4. _____	4. _____	4. _____
5. _____	5. _____	5. _____
6. _____	6. _____	6. _____
7. _____	7. _____	7. _____
8. _____	8. _____	8. _____
9. _____	9. _____	9. _____
10. _____	10. _____	10. _____

Class _____   Name_____

11. _____	11. _____	11. _____
12. _____	12. _____	12. _____
13. _____	13. _____	13. _____
14. _____	14. _____	14. _____
15. _____	15. _____	15. _____
16. _____	16. _____	16. _____
17. _____	17. _____	17. _____
18. _____	18. _____	18. _____
19. _____	19. _____	19. _____
20. _____	20. _____	20. _____
21. _____	21. _____	21. _____
22. _____	22. _____	22. _____
23. _____	23. _____	23. _____
24. _____	24. _____	24. _____

Describe any differences between your perceived self and the ways your reviewers perceived you (your presenting selves). What factors contribute to the differences in perception? Whose view is the most accurate and why?

_____

_____

_____

_____

_____

Why might your reviewers in this exercise view you differently from the way you perceive yourself? Would other people in your life view you like either of the people in this exercise? Give some specific examples with reasons why they would or would not have a similar perception.

_____

_____

_____

_____

Class _____   Name_____

2.3 EGO BOOSTERS AND BUSTERS

Activity Type: Invitation to Insight/Group Activity

PURPOSES

1. To identify how significant others have shaped your self-concept.
2. To realize how you may shape the self-concept of others.

INSTRUCTIONS

1. In the appropriate spaces below describe the actions of several "ego boosters": significant others who shaped your self-concept in a positive way. Also describe the behavior of "ego busters" who contributed to a more negative self-concept.
2. Next, recall several incidents in which you behaved as an ego booster or buster to others. Not all ego boosters and busters are obvious. Include in your description several incidents in which the messages were **subtle or nonverbal**.
3. Summarize the lessons you have learned from this experience by answering the questions at the end of this exercise.

EGO BOOSTER MESSAGES YOU HAVE RECEIVED

EXAMPLE

I perceive(d) _my communication lab partner_ **(significant other)** as telling me I am/was

attractive **(self-concept element**) when he or she kept _sneaking glances at me and smiling during_

our taping project.

1. I perceived _____ (significant other) as telling me I am/was

   _____ (self-concept element) when he/she _____

   _____

   _____

2. I perceived _____ (significant other) as telling me I am/was

   _____ (self-concept element) when he/she _____

   _____

   _____

EGO BUSTER MESSAGES YOU HAVE RECEIVED

EXAMPLE

I perceive(d) _my neighbor_ (significant other) as telling me I am/was _not an important friend_ (self-concept element) when he/she _had a big party last weekend and didn't invite me._

Class _____   Name_____

1.   I perceived _____ (significant other) as telling me I am/was

              _____(self-concept element) when he/she _____

              _____

              _____

2.   I perceived _____ (significant other) as telling me I am/was

              _____(self-concept element) when he/she _____

              _____

              _____

EGO BOOSTER MESSAGES YOU HAVE SENT

EXAMPLE

I was a booster to _my instructor_ when I _told her I enjoyed last Tuesday's lecture._

1.   I was a booster to _____ when I _____

              _____

              _____

2.   I was a booster to _____ when I _____

              _____

              _____

EGO BUSTER MESSAGES YOU HAVE SENT

EXAMPLE

I was a buster to _my sister_ when I _forgot to phone her or send even a card on her birthday._

1.   I was a buster to _____ when I _____

              _____

2.   I was a buster to _____ when I _____

              _____

              _____

CONCLUSIONS

Who are the people who have most influenced your self-concept in the past? What messages did each one send to influence you so strongly?

_____

_____

_____

_____

What people are the greatest influences on your self-concept now? Is each person a positive or a negative influence? What messages does each one send to influence your self-concept?

_____

_____

_____

_____

Who are the people whom *you* have influenced greatly? What messages have you sent to each one about his or her self-concept? How have you sent these messages?

_____

_____

_____

_____

What ego booster or buster messages do you want to send to the important people in your life? How (with what channels) can you send each one?

_____

_____

_____

Class _____   Name_____

GROUP DISCUSSION

After completing the first part of this activity individually, share some of your answers with a small group of classmates Then, as a group, answer the questions below.

1. What channels are most important for you to receive ego boosters? or buster messages do you want to send to the important people in your life? How (with what channels) can you send each one?

_____

_____

_____

2. What channels are most often used for ego busters that are unintentional? What advice would you have in order to avoid inadvertently sending ego busters?

_____

_____

_____

3. After reviewing your experiences, what advice would you give to supervisors regarding ego boosters and ego busters?

_____

_____

_____

4. After reviewing your experiences, what advice would you give to parents regarding ego boosters and ego busters?

_____

_____

_____

2.4 REEVALUATING YOUR "CAN'TS"
ACTIVITY TYPE: INVITATION TO INSIGHT

PURPOSE

To identify and eliminate self-fulfilling prophecies which hamper effective communication.

INSTRUCTIONS

1. Complete the following lists by describing communication-related difficulties you have in the following areas.
2. After filling in each blank space, follow the starred instructions that follow the list (*).

DIFFICULTIES YOU HAVE COMMUNICATING WITH FAMILY MEMBERS

EXAMPLES

I can't *discuss politics with my dad without having an argument* because *he's so set in his ways.*
I can't *tell my brother how much I love him* because *I'll feel foolish.* _____

1. I can't _____

   because _____

2. I can't _____

   because _____

* Corrections (see instructions at end of exercise)

_____

DIFFICULTIES YOU HAVE COMMUNICATING WITH PEOPLE AT SCHOOL OR AT WORK

EXAMPLES

I can't *say "no" when my boss asks me to work overtime*
because *he'll fire me.*
I can't *participate in class discussions even when I know the answers or have a question*
because *I just freeze up.* _____

1. I can't _____

   because _____

2. I can't _____

   because _____

* Corrections (see instructions at end of exercise)

_____

_____

DIFFICULTIES YOU HAVE COMMUNICATING WITH STRANGERS

EXAMPLES

I can't *start a conversation with someone I've never met before*
because *I'll look stupid.*
I can't *ask smokers to move or stop smoking*
because *they'll get mad.*

1. I can't _____

   because _____

2. I can't _____

   because _____

* Corrections (see instructions at end of exercise)

_____

_____

DIFFICULTIES YOU HAVE COMMUNICATING WITH FRIENDS

EXAMPLES

I can't *find the courage to ask my friend to repay the money he owes me*
because *I'm afraid he'll question our friendship.*
I can't *say no when friends ask me to do favors and I'm busy*
because *I'm afraid they'll think I'm not their friend.*

1. I can't _____

   because _____

2. I can't _____

   because _____

* Corrections (see instructions at end of exercise)

_____

_____

DIFFICULTIES YOU HAVE COMMUNICATING WITH YOUR ROMANTIC PARTNER (PAST OF PRESENT)

EXAMPLES

I can't *tell Bill to wear a tie to the party*
because *he'll laugh at me.*
I can't *bring up going to visit my parents*
because *we'll fight.*

1. I can't _____

   because _____

Class _____   Name_____

2. I can't _____

   because _____

* Corrections (see instructions at end of exercise)

_____

PREDICTIONS MADE BY OTHERS

EXAMPLES

You'll never amount to anything.   You can't expect much with your background.
You're just like your father.   The James children never were too bright.

1. _____

2. _____

* Corrections (see instructions at end of exercise)

_____

*After you have completed the list, continue as follows:
   a. Read the list you have made. Actually say each item to yourself and note your feelings.
   b. Now read the list again, but with a slight difference. For each "can't," substitute the word "won't" or "until now I've chosen not to." For instance, "I can't say no to friends' requests" becomes "I won't say no" or "Until now I've chosen not to say no." Circle any statements that are actually "won'ts" or choices.
   c. Read the list for a third time. For this repetition substitute "I don't know how" or "I haven't yet learned to" for your original "can't." Instead of saying "I can't approach strangers," say, "I don't know how to approach strangers." *Correct* your original list to show which statements are truly "don't know how" or "haven't yet learned" statements
   d. For the "Predictions made by others," substitute your strength(s) which makes the prediction untrue (example: "I am my father's child, but I can choose not to repeat behaviors he has that I don't like.").

After completing this exercise, consider how greater awareness of the power that negative self-fulfilling prophecies have on your self-concept and thus on your communication behavior. Imagine how differently you would behave if you eliminated any incorrect uses of the word "can't" from your thinking.

2.5 SUCCESS IN MANAGING IMPRESSIONS

Activity Type: Skill Builder

PURPOSES

1. To acknowledge at least one successful aspect of self that you have revealed to others and one that you might improve upon.
2. To reflect on your level of self-monitoring in that instance.

INSTRUCTIONS

1. Individually or in groups, describe one instance in which you successfully presented yourself to another person. Describe how you managed that impression of yourself. It may be a significant impression (you got a job you wanted or a date you wanted) or it may be an ongoing, slowly made success (you were a better parent this week or you kept your cool with your roommate during last week's conflict). Describe how you managed manner, setting and/or appearance to create the impression you wanted.
2. Describe how aware you were of your own behaviors: whether you had high or low self-monitoring, and how effective or ineffective your level of monitoring was for the impression management situation.
3. Now repeat the process with a less successful self you presented. Again describe manner, setting, appearance and level of self-monitoring. With this face, describe what you could do to be more successful in identity management.

A. The successful self I revealed to others

_____

_____

_____

How I managed the impression:

Manner _____

_____

Setting _____

_____

Appearance _____

_____

Effectiveness of self-monitoring (level of awareness)

_____

_____

_____

Class _____   Name_____

B. The less successful self I revealed to others

_____

_____

_____

How I managed the impression:

Manner_____

_____

Setting _____

_____

Appearance _____

_____

Effectiveness of self-monitoring (level of awareness)

_____

_____

_____

How I might have improved on this identity management:

_____

_____

_____

2.6 MEDIATED MESSAGES – IDENTITY MANAGEMENT

Activity Type: Group Discussion

PURPOSE

To analyze your presentation of self in mediated communication. Mediated communication involves any extension of our communication abilities (writing, phoning, IMing, etc.).

INSTRUCTIONS

Discuss each of the questions below in your group. For each question, take a minute of silence and let each person jot down some notes. Then go around and let each person share something. Then have a more extended discussion and if directed by your instructor, prepare to report your groups conclusions back to the whole class.

1. Describe ways in which messages from the mass media (i.e., music, television, film, magazines, books) have contributed to your self-concept or the self-concepts of people you know well.

   _____

   _____

2. Your text states that people often prefer mediated channels when their self-presentation is threatened (delivering bad news, declining invitations). Do your experiences refute or validate this conclusion? Give examples.

   _____

   _____

3. Identity management is important in mediated contexts. Describe how you manage identity in any mediated contexts you use (online dating services, written notes, email, e-mail address, instant messaging, blogging, personal ads, web pages).

   _____

   _____

4. Do you prefer to meet people online or face-to-face initially? Why? Is your answer the same or different for friendships than for work or career situations? Why?

   _____

   _____

   _____

   _____

2.7 YOUR CALL–IDENTITY MANAGEMENT
Activity Type: Group Discussion

PURPOSES

1. To analyze the presentation of self in a communication situation.
2. To highlight self-fulfilling prophecies that may help or hinder a communication transaction.

INSTRUCTIONS

Use the case below and the discussion questions that follow to discuss the variety of communication issues involved in effective communication. Make notes on this page, add other pages on your own, or prepare a group report/analysis based on your discussion. Add your own experiences to individualize the analysis to make it **Your Call**.

CASE

Hiroshi was hired in an entry-level position one month ago at a brokerage firm. He wants to succeed at this firm, but is worried that he won't be able fit in with most of the others who have Ivy League degrees and Fifth Avenue wardrobes. Hiroshi's boss graduated from a state college, though, and is very successful at this firm.   One of Hiroshi's fellow-workers has just invited him to join a few people from work at a bar on Friday evening.

1. If Hiroshi joins the group at the bar, what types of manner, setting and appearance could contribute to the impression he wants to make?

_____

_____

2. Explain how Hiroshi's social comparison may affect his self-esteem and his communication.

_____

_____

3. What self-fulfilling prophecies might affect Hiroshi's success in this situation?

_____

_____

4. How would you recommend Hiroshi manage his identity at work to present himself effectively? Cite reasons for your recommendations.

_____

_____

_____

_____

STUDY GUIDE

CROSSWORD PUZZLE

ACROSS

1. characteristic ways that you think and behave across a variety of situations
3. the part of the self-concept that involves evaluations of self-worth
5. a self-concept that is highly dependent on belonging to a group, common in cultures where the main desire is to build connections between the self and others
6. other whose opinion is important enough to affect one's self-concept strongly
7. information about past successes or failures that no longer hold true   the image a person presents to others
8. the process of observing one's behavior and using these observations to shape the way one behaves
10. the self whom we believe ourselves to be in moments of candor
12. a prophecy about an event that makes the outcome more likely to occur than would otherwise have been the case
13. a self-concept that is strong "I" oriented, common in cultures where the main desire is to promote the self

DOWN

2. the relatively stable set of perceptions that each individual holds of himself or herself
4. the self a person shows to others
6. comparison of oneself to others
9. another name for the presenting self
11. groups against which we compare ourselves, thereby influencing our self-concept and self-esteem

TRUE/FALSE

Mark the statements below as true or false. Correct statements that are false on the lines below to create a true statement.

_____ 1. Collaboration in identity management means absolute agreement about each person's role.

_____ 2. Most researchers agree that we are born with a fully formed self-concept.

_____ 3. Some studies show that people strongly influenced by media body images develop more negative self-images.

_____ 4. People who dislike themselves are likely to believe that others won't like them either.

_____ 5. Research has shown that people with high self-esteem seek out partners who view them unfavorably because they are strong enough to take the criticism.

_____ 6. Luckily, your self-concept is not affected by the language that you speak.

_____ 7. In individualistic societies, there is a higher degree of communication apprehension.

_____ 8. The self-concept is such a powerful force that it not only influences how you see yourself in the present but also can actually influence your future behavior and that of others.

_____   9.   Research shows that people who believe they are incompetent are more likely than others to pursue rewarding relationships in an attempt to ally themselves with competent people.

_____

_____   10.   The communication strategies we use to influence how others view us are all conscious behaviors.

_____

COMPLETION

Fill in the blanks below with the correct terms chosen from the list below.

distorted feedback   obsolete information   self-delusion
ego booster   ego buster   realistic expectations
realistic perceptions   manner   setting
appearance

1.   _____ is someone who helps enhance your self-esteem by acting in ways that make you feel accepted, important and loved.

2.   _____ is someone who acts to reduce your self-esteem.

3.   _____ are messages that others send to you that are unrealistically positive or negative.

4.   _____ consists of a communicator's words and nonverbal actions that help create an impression.

5.   _____ is information that was once true about you that is no longer true.

6.   _____ are the personal items people use to shape an image.

7.   _____ is the inability to see a real need for change in the self due to holding an unrealistically favorable picture of yourself.

8.   _____ are reasonable goals to set for self-growth.

9.   _____ refers to the physical items we use to influence how others view us.

10. _____ are relatively accurate views of the strengths and weaknesses of the self.

MULTIPLE CHOICE

Identify which principle influences the self-concept in each example.

a. obsolete information
b. distorted feedback
c. emphasis on perfection
d. social expectations

_____ 1. You always scored more points than anyone else on your team in high school. You still think you're the best even though your college teammates are scoring more than you.

_____ 2. You keep getting down on yourself because you can't cook as well as Megan, even though you are a great student and a fair athlete.

_____ 3. You believe people shouldn't brag or boast, so you tell others that you "blew" the chemistry test and got a "C–" but you never acknowledge your "A's" in math.

_____ 4. Your parents tell you, their friends, and all your relatives about all your wonderful accomplishments, even though you have only average achievement.

_____ 5. Janee says that you are insensitive to her perspective despite your many attempts to listen honestly to her and empathize.

_____ 6. You pay a lot of attention to the magazines showing perfectly dressed and groomed individuals and keep wishing you could look as good as they do.

_____ 7. You think of yourself as the shy fifth grader despite being at the social hub of at least three clubs on campus.

_____ 8. You feel uncomfortable accepting the compliments your friends honestly give you.

_____ 9. You're exhausted by trying to get all A's, work 30 hours a week, and be a loving romantic partner at the same time. You don't see how so many other people manage to get it all done.

_____ 10. "You're the perfect weight," your father tells you despite your recent gain of twenty pounds over the normal weight for your height.

Choose the *best* answer for each statement below:

11. Deciding which part of your self-concept to reveal to others is termed
    a. prophecy.
    b. impression management.
    c. collectivism.
    d. two-faced syndrome.

12. The most significant part of a person's self-concept
    a. is the social roles the person plays.
    b. is his or her appearance.
    c. is his or her accomplishments.
    d. is different for different people.

13. A sense of identity begins
    a. at 30.
    b. with the start of pre-school or school
    c. very early in life.
    d. at the onset of puberty.

14. Which of the following could be an example of a self-fulfilling prophecy?
    a. Sid is born with a very large nose.
    b. Margarita has a very large, extended family.

    c. Serge is a Russian immigrant.
    d. Joy has given up on trying to talk to her unreasonable father.

15. The fact that none of us can see ourselves completely accurately illustrates the _____ nature of the self-concept.
    a. subjective
    b. objective
    c. unrealistic
    d. verification

16. Personality traits
    a. are a matter of degree
    b. are an either-or matter
    c. determine all of our communication-related behavior
    d. tend to change more as we grow older

17. The influence of significant others
    a. is the sole determinant of our self-concept
    b. becomes less powerful as people grow older
    c. is synonymous with the term reflected appraisal
    d. only occurs in people with poor self-concepts

18. Computer-mediated communication
    a. makes it impossible to manage identity
    b. has only disadvantages for impression management
    c. can be an effective tool for impression management
    d. always lessens the amount of interpersonal communication.

19. Which is the fourth stage of a self-fulfilling prophecy?
    a. Holding an expectation (for yourself or for others)
    b. Behaving in accordance with that expectation
    c. The expectation coming to pass
    d. Reinforcing the original expectation

20. Communicating ego busters to others would seem to most violate which concept of moral rules theory?
    a. Nonmaleficence
    b. Self-improvement
    c. Justice
    d. Gratitude

CHAPTER 2 STUDY GUIDE ANSWERS

CROSSWORD PUZZLE

The completed crossword contains the following answers:

- 1. personality
- 2. self-concept (down)
- 3. self-esteem
- 4. presenting (down)
- 5. collective
- 6. significant / social (down)
- 7. obsolete
- 8. self-monitoring / self (down)
- 9. facade (down)
- 10. perceived / preference (down)
- 12. self-fulfilling
- 13. individualistic

TRUE/FALSE

1. F	5. F	9. F
2. T	6. F	10. F
3. T	7. F	
4. T	8. T	

COMPLETION

1. ego booster	5. obsolete information	9. setting
2. ego buster	6. appearance	10. realistic perceptions
3. distorted feedback	7. self-delusion	
4. manner	8. realistic expectations	

41

MULTIPLE CHOICE

1.	a	5.	b	9.	c	13.	c	17.	b
2.	c	6.	c	10.	b	14.	d	18.	c
3.	d	7.	a	11.	b	15.	a	19.	d
4	b	8.	d	12.	d	16.	a	20.	a

C H A P T E R   T H R E E

Perception: What You See Is What You Get

OUTLINE

Use this outline to take notes as you read the chapter in the text and/or as your instructor lectures in class.

I. **THE PERCEPTION PROCESS**
   A. **Selection** is influenced by
      1. Intense stimuli
      2. Repetitious stimuli
      3. Contrast or change in stimulation
      4. Motives

   B. **Organization**
      1. Figure–ground organization
      2. Perceptual schema
         a. Appearance
         b. Social roles
         c. Interaction style
         d. Psychological traits
         e. Membership
      3. Stereotyping
      4. Punctuation
   C. **Interpretation**
      1. Degree of involvement with the other person
      2. Personal experience
      3. Assumptions about human behavior
      4. Attitudes
      5. Expectations
      6. Knowledge
      7. Self-concept
      8. Relational satisfaction
   D. **Negotiation**
      1. Narratives tell our stories
      2. Narratives may clash
      2. Narratives may enhance relationships

II. **INFLUENCES ON PERCEPTION**
   A. **Physiological Influences**
      1. Senses

2. Age
3. Health
4. Fatigue
5. Hunger
6. Biological Cycles
7. Psychological Challeges

B. Cultural Differences
1. World view
2. Value of talk and silence
3. Ethnocentrism
4. Geography

C. Social Roles
1. Gender Roles (masculine, feminine, androgynous, undifferentiated)
2. Occupational Roles
   a. careers
   b. Zimbardo experiment

D. Self-Concept
1. Judgments of others
2. Judgments of self

III. COMMON TENDENCIES IN PERCEPTION
A. We Judge Ourselves More Charitably Than Others
B. We Pay More Attention to Others' Negative Characteristics
C. We Are Influenced by the Obvious
D. We Cling to First Impressions (halo/devil effect)
E. We Assume Others Are Similar to Us

IV. PERCEPTION CHECKING
A. Elements of Perception Checking
1. Describe behavior
2. Interpret behavior two ways
3. Request clarification

B. Perception-Checking Considerations
1. Completeness
2. Nonverbal congruency
3. Cultural rules
   a. Low-context cultures
   b. High-context cultures
4. Face saving

V. EMPATHY AND COMMUNICATION
A. Definition
1. Empathy—ability to re-create another's perspective
   a. Perspective taking
   b. Emotional dimension

         c.   Genuine concern
      2.   Sympathy — compassion for another's predicament from your point of view

B. The Pillow Method — A Tool for Building Empathy
      1.   Position One: I'm right, you're wrong
      2.   Position Two: You're right, I'm wrong
      3.   Position Three: Both right, both wrong
      4.   Position Four: The issue isn't as important as it seems
      5.   Conclusion: There is truth in all four perspectives

KEY TERMS

androgynous	organization
attribution	perception checking
empathy	pillow method
ethnocentrism	punctuation
gender role	selection
halo effect	self-serving bias
interpretation	stereotyping
narrative	sympathy
negotiation	

ACTIVITIES

3.1 GUARDING AGAINST PERCEPTUAL ERRORS
Activity Type: Invitation to Insight

PURPOSES

1. To identify potentially distorted opinions you have formed about people.
2. To recognize some perceptual errors that may have contributed to those distorted opinions.

INSTRUCTIONS

1. Identify two people about whom you've formed strong opinions. These opinions can be positive or negative. In either case, describe them.
2. Using the checklist provided, comment on the accuracy or inaccuracy of your perceptions of each person. See Chapter 3 of *Looking Out/Looking In* for a more detailed description of the checklist factors. NOTE: Not every factor may apply to each person.
3. Record your conclusions at the end of the exercise.
4. Compare your examples with those of other classmates.

	Example	PERSON A	PERSON B
Identify each person. Describe your opinions.	Joni is my wife's good friend. I don't like her; I think she's boring. Her voice is shrill, and I find her annoying.		
1. We judge ourselves more charitably than others.	When Joni lost her job, I thought it was Joni's fault because she's so annoying. Of course, when I got laid off a few months later, I blamed the economy and mentioned nothing about my performance or personality.		
2. We pay more attention to other's negative characteristics.	Joni is attractive, intelligent, successful, and athletic. I tend to disregard all those positive qualities and focus on her shrill voice.		

Class_____   Name _____

3. We are influenced by the obvious.	Because she's my wife's friend, Joni is around a lot, so I probably notice her voice or her calls more than is usual.		
4. We cling to first impressions.	I haven't liked Joni from the beginning. She would call right at our dinner time. Even though she doesn't do this any more, I still remember it and I'm sure it influences my opinion of her.		
5. We tend to assume that others are similar to us.	I just assume that Joni will know when I don't want her around. I assume she'd be interested in things I'm interested in. Perhaps she finds the topics I talk about boring, too.		

CONCLUSIONS

Based on the observations above, how accurate or inaccurate are your perceptions of other people?

_____

_____

_____

_____

What might you do in the future to guard against inaccurate perceptions of people?

_____

_____

_____

_____

3.2 EXAMINING YOUR INTERPRETATIONS

Activity Type: Invitation to Insight

PURPOSES

1. To identify interpretations you make about others' behavior in your important interpersonal relationships.
2. To recognize perceptual factors influencing those interpretations.
3. To assess the validity of your interpretations.

INTRODUCTION

There are many ways to interpret what another person says or does. For example, you may notice that a new classmate is wearing a cross necklace and imagine that she is a religious person, or you might notice that a friend isn't making much eye contact with you and assume that he is not telling you the truth. We usually assume that our interpretations are accurate. In fact, these assumptions might be incorrect and different from how others see themselves.

INSTRUCTIONS

1. For the next few days, observe two people important to you and record your interpretations of each.
2. After completing this, assess the context and the other person and consider sharing your observations with each person involved and see if your interpretations match theirs.

EXAMPLE

Name *Stan Morris*_____   context *Neighbor and friend*_____

A. Describe an assumption about this person's thoughts or feelings.
    I've been thinking that Stan is mad at me, probably because I've been asking so many favors of him lately.

B. Describe at least two items of behavior (things the person has said or done) that lead you to believe your assumption about this person's thoughts or feelings is accurate.
    1. *When I asked to borrow his backpacking gear he said yes, but he mentioned several times how much it cost him.*
    2. *When I asked him for a ride to school last week when my car was in the shop, he said OK but didn't talk much and drove more quickly than usual.*

C. Give at least two reasons why your assumption about this person's thoughts or feelings may *not* be accurate. (You may ask the person you are observing for help.)

    1. *Stan is often moody. Even if he is upset, it may not be because of anything I've said or done.*
    2. *I'm often hard on myself, taking the blame for anything that goes wrong. Perhaps I'm doing that here, and Stan doesn't mind doing me the favors.*

D. Which of the following factors influenced your perception of this person? Explain how each of these factors affected the accuracy or inaccuracy of your interpretations.
    Physiological influences
    Social roles (gender, occupation) Perhaps my being a woman has something to do with my self-doubt. I often wonder if I'm being too "forward" in asking a man for favors.
    Cultural differences
    Self-concept. *I often view myself as less desirable as a friend than other people I know. I*

Class_____   Name _____

think this leads me to interpret others' reactions as confirmations of my worst fears,
whether or not those fears are valid.

PERSON 1

Name _____   Context _____

A. Describe an assumption you have made about this person's thoughts or feelings.

_____

_____

B. Describe at least two items of behavior (things the person has said or done) that lead you to
    believe your assumption about this person's thoughts or feelings is accurate.

1. _____

_____

2. _____

_____

C. Give at least two reasons why your assumption about this person's thoughts or feelings
    may *not* be accurate. (You may ask the person you are observing for help.)

1. _____

_____

_____

2. _____

_____

_____

D. Which of the following factors influence your perception of this person? Explain how each
    of these factors affected the accuracy or inaccuracy of your interpretations.

Physiological influences _____

_____

Social roles (gender, occupation) _____

_____

Cultural differences _____

_____

Self-concept _____

Class_____   Name _____

PERSON 2

Name _____   Context _____

A.   Describe an assumption you have made about this person's thoughts or feelings.

_____

_____

B.   Describe at least two items of behavior (things the person has said or done) that lead you to believe your assumption about this person's thoughts or feelings is accurate.

1.   _____

_____

2.   _____

_____

C.   Give at least two reasons why your assumption about this person's thoughts or feelings may *not* be accurate. (You may ask the person you are observing for help.)

1.   _____

_____

_____

2.   _____

_____

_____

D.   Which of the following factors influenced your perception of this person? Explain how each of these factors affected the accuracy or inaccuracy of your interpretations.

Physiological influences _____

_____

Social roles (gender, occupation) _____

_____

Cultural differences _____

_____

Self-concept _____

_____

3.3 SHIFTING PERSPECTIVES (PILLOW METHOD)

Activity Type: Invitation to Insight/ Group Activity

PURPOSES

1. To understand how others view an interpersonal issue.
2. To recognize the merits and drawbacks of each person's perspective.
3. To perceive an issue from multiple perspectives

INSTRUCTIONS

1. Select one disagreement or other issue that is now affecting an interpersonal relationship. This might be an issue such as "I think our children should go to public school; my spouse wants them to go to private school" or a more public disagreement such as "I think voting for a third party helps democracy in our country; my friend thinks it undermines democracy by drawing votes away from the two major parties."
2. Record enough background information for an outsider to understand your stance on the issue. Who is involved? How long has the disagreement been going on? What are the basic issues involved?
3. Describe the issue from each of the four positions listed below.
4. Record your conclusions at the end of this exercise.

OPTIONS

Create diverse groups of four; try to have gender, age, and ethnic diversity if possible. Let each person jot down a few notes about a disagreement and the four positions. Now, have one person at a time describe his/her situation and the first position. For each of the other positions, the other group members can help the speaker see even more ways to view the situation from other perspectives.

With a partner, role-play your situation orally for the class.

Brief Background Information

_____

_____

_____

_____

Position 1: "I'm right and you're wrong." Explain how you are right and the other person is wrong.

_____

_____

_____

_____

_____

_____

Position 2: "You're right and I'm wrong." Explain how the other person's position is correct, or at least understandable.

_____

_____

_____

_____

_____

Position 3: "We're both right and we're both wrong." Show that there are both correct (or understandable) and mistaken (or unreasonable) parts of both positions.

_____

_____

_____

_____

_____

Position 4: "The issue may be less important than it seems; some other things may be more important." Describe at least two ways in which the elements developed in positions 1–3 might affect your relationship. Describe at least one way in which the issue might be seen as *less* important than it was originally and describe at least one way in which the issue might be seen as *more* important than it was originally.

_____

_____

_____

_____

_____

CONCLUSION

1. Explain how there is some truth in each of the preceding positions.

_____

_____

2. Explain how viewing the issue from each of the preceding positions might change your perception of the issue and how it might change your behavior in the future.

_____

_____

_____

3. Explain how this issue and your **understanding** of it affect your relationship.

_____

_____

4. Explain the impact of hearing classmates explain how you might view the issue differently.

_____

_____

3.4 PERCEPTION CHECKING AND OTHER OPTIONS

Activity Type: Skill Builder/Group Activity

PURPOSES

1. To report your observations of another person clearly and accurately.
2. To report at least two interpretations to another person.
3. To discuss and evaluate the various choices you have available to you when dealing with perceptual problems.

INSTRUCTIONS

1. As a group, detail three situations below in which there are potential perceptual problems.
2. Use the form below to record behavior for each relationship listed.
3. For each example of behavior, record two plausible interpretations.
4. Record a request for feedback.
5. With others in the group, rehearse how you could share with the person in question each example of behavior and the possible interpretations you have developed.
6. Evaluate the various other options you have to check out perceptions. Describe the probable outcome of each.

EXAMPLE

Perceptual problem: *Jill is annoyed by her math professor who calls on her for answers and trys to get her involved more in the class. Jill is uncomfortable about this, but she is afraid that the professor might pay even more attention to her if she brings it up.*

Perception checking opening: *Professor Smith, I'm confused about something.*

Behavior: *I've noticed that you call on me quite often — at least once each class, whether or not I raise my hand.*

Interpretation A: *Sometimes I wonder if you're trying to catch me unprepared.*

Interpretation B: *On the other hand, sometimes I think you're trying to challenge me by forcing me to keep on my toes.*

Request for feedback: *Can you tell me why you call on me so often?*

Perception checking options

1. *Jill could do nothing. Perhaps it would be better to wait and see if she has been imagining this by watching a bit more.*
2. *Jill could start initiating answers herself and see if Professor Smith changes behavior.*
3. *Jill could just tell the Prof that she doesn't like being called on. This might alienate her in the Prof's eyes, however, and might affect her grade.*
4. *Jill could just ask if the Prof was trying to embarrass her. We thought the Prof might not know what Jill was referring to, though, if she didn't describe behavior. The Prof probably teaches hundreds of students and might not realize what's going on in Jill's eyes.*
5. *Jill could do the complete perception checking statement we wrote above. Our group thought this has a good chance for success if the Prof didn't get defensive. If Jill could deliver the statement in a non-defensive tone and then follow it up with how much she likes the class, perhaps the Prof would realize how much Jill is bothered.*

Class_____   Name _____

SITUATION ONE

Perceptual problem: _____

_____

_____

Perception-checking opening: _____

   Behavior: _____

   Interpretation A: _____

   Interpretation B: _____

   Request for feedback: _____

Perception-checking options:

1. _____

2. _____

3. _____

SITUATION TWO

Perceptual problem: _____

_____

_____

Perception-checking opening: _____

   Behavior: _____

   Interpretation A: _____

   Interpretation B: _____

   Request for feedback: _____

Perception-checking options:

1. _____

2. _____

3. _____

Class_____   Name _____

SITUATION THREE

Perceptual problem: _____

_____

_____

Perception-checking opening: _____

   Behavior: _____

   Interpretation A: _____

   Interpretation B: _____

   Request for feedback: _____

Perception-checking options:

1. _____

2. _____

3. _____

3.5 PERCEPTION-CHECKING PRACTICE

Activity Type: Skill Builder

PURPOSE

To create effective perception-checking statements.

INSTRUCTIONS

1. Alone or with a partner, write a perception check for each of the situations below or spontaneously create an oral perception check. If you write them first, practice delivering them aloud to each other. Evaluation Form 3.7 is useful to rate each other's delivery.

EXAMPLE

Yesterday your friend Erin laughed at a joke about "dumb blonds." You found it offensive.

Perception-checking statement *Erin, when Joey cracked the dumb blond joke last night, you laughed. I'm wondering if you disapproved of the joke but laughed just to make Joey feel comfortable, or if you really think that blonds are not as smart as the rest of the population. Can you clarify things for me?*

1. Last night you saw a recent date walking on the beach, holding hands with someone. You'd like to date again, but don't want to if a current relationship exists. You get a call from the recent date, asking you to a movie and dinner this weekend.

   _____

   _____

   _____

2. Ever since the school year began, your father has called weekly, asking how you are doing. He's just called and asked again.

   _____

   _____

   _____

3. Your friend was driving you home from a party last night when he began to weave the car between lanes on the highway. You were uncomfortable, but didn't say anything then. Now it is the next morning and he shows up to take you to a class. You have decided to bring up the incident.

   _____

   _____

   _____

4. For the last two weeks, when you are leaving your house, your roommate has asked for a ride somewhere. Your roommate has a car, but you haven't seen it lately. You are in a hurry now, and your roommate has just asked for another ride.

   _____

_____

_____

5. You return home at night to find your roommate reading on the couch. When you walk into the room and greet him, he grunts and turns his face away from you and keeps reading.

_____

_____

_____

6. Last week your instructor returned your exam with a low grade and the comment, "This kind of work paints a bleak picture for the future." You have approached the instructor to discuss the remark.

_____

_____

_____

7. In one of your regular long distance phone conversations you ask your favorite cousin about his romantic life. He sighs and says, "Oh, it's OK, I guess."

_____

_____

_____

8. Your girl or boyfriend (or spouse) announces that she or he plans to spend next Friday night with friends from work. You usually spend Friday nights with each other.

_____

_____

_____

9. Last week your supervisor at work, Ms. Black, gave you a big assignment. Three times since then she has asked you whether you're having any trouble with it.

_____

_____

_____

10. Last weekend your next-door neighbor, Steve, raked a big pile of leaves near your property line, promising to clean them up after work on Monday. It's Wednesday, and the wind is blowing the leaves into your yard.

_____

_____

_____

11. One of your classmates sits by you every day in class and you've done a lot of homework together; he's called you at home a few times a week. He suggests that you meet for dinner this weekend.

_____

_____

_____

12. You've noticed one of your office mates looking over at you a number of times during the past few days. At first she looked away quickly, but now she smiles every time you look up and catch her looking at you. You've been under a lot of pressure at work lately and have been extremely busy. You can't understand why she keeps looking at you. You've decided to ask.

_____

_____

_____

3.6 PERCEPTION CHECKING

Activity Type: Oral Skill

PURPOSE

To evaluate your skill at using perception-checking statements.

INSTRUCTIONS

1. Identify a situation in your life in which a perception check might be appropriate. Describe the situation to the person who will be evaluating your skill. Possible topics: controversial issues, things that "bug" you, perceived injustices, personal dilemmas, and misperceptions.
2. Deliver a complete perception check to your evaluator, without using notes, following the criteria listed in Chapter 3 of *Looking Out/Looking In* and outlined in the checklist below.

CHECKLIST

_____ Describes background for potential perception-checking situation.

_____ Delivers complete perception check

      _____ Reports at least one behavior that **describes,** without evaluating or judging, what the person has said or done.

      _____ States two interpretations that are distinctly different, equally probable, and are based on the reported behavior.

      _____ Makes a sincere request for feedback clarifying how to interpret the reported behavior.

_____ Verbal and nonverbal behavior

      _____ Reflects sincere desire for clarification of the perception.

      _____ Sounds realistic and consistent with style of the speaker.

      _____ Uses nonthreatening, nondefensive voice and eye contact.

_____ Realistically and clearly assesses how perception checking and other alternatives can be used in everyday life.

      _____ In situation described here.

      _____ In other situations (be specific).

Class_____   Name _____

1. Describe how well perception checking might (or might not) work in the situation you have chosen. If you do not think a complete perception check is the best approach for this situation, explain why and describe a more promising alternative.

_____

_____

_____

2. Describe various channels you can use for perception-checking.

_____

_____

_____

3. What is the impact on the person using a perception check of having to think of more than one possible interpretation?

_____

_____

4. What is the impact on the person hearing the perception check of hearing more than one possible interpretation?

_____

_____

_____

5. What would you predict are some long and short term effects on relationships in which people use more perception checks? Consider employee/employer, parent/child, and co-workers, friends and partners.

_____

_____

_____

_____

3.7 MEDIATED MESSAGES – PERCEPTION

Activity Type: Group Discussion

PURPOSE

To investigate perceptual differences in mediated communication.

INSTRUCTIONS

Discuss each of the questions below in your group. Prepare written answers for your instructor, or be prepared to contribute to a large group discussion, comparing your experiences with those of others in your class.

1. Think of ways in which messages sent through mediated messages may contribute to misperceptions. (Example: *I called my grandmother and she thought my tone of voice sounded like I was irritated with her; she didn't say anything to me at the time, but complained to my mother about me.*)

    _____

    _____

    _____

2. How do the influences on perception (physiological or cultural differences, social roles, self-concept) affect these mediated misperceptions? (Example: *Physiological: I was tired when I called my grandmother and I know she has age-related hearing problems*)

    _____

    _____

3. Prepare a perception-checking statement that could be used in a mediated context. Specify the mediated channel and the likelihood of success of the perception-checking attempt. (Example: *"When you said in your last e-mail that you were busy on Saturday, I wondered if you had a previous commitment or if you were irritated with me for some reason I'm not aware of and so don't want to see me. What did you mean?" I think this perception-checking statement gives my partner a way to bring up anything that might be wrong, so it has a good likelihood of success.*)

    _____

    _____

    _____

4. Are there times when using perception checks in mediated contexts might be preferable to using them face-to-face? Explain.   Are there times when perception checks in mediated contexts might be less effective or appropriate? Explain.

    _____

    _____

    _____

3.8 YOUR CALL – PERCEPTION
Activity Type: Group Discussion

PURPOSES

1. To explain perceptual factors that may contribute to misunderstandings.
2. To use perception checking to clarify the situation.

INSTRUCTIONS

Use the following case to explore the variety of communication issues involved in communication and perception.

CASE

Jorge is a registered nurse at a facility that cares for about 80 elderly patients. Jorge has been at the facility longer than any of the other nurses and has his choice of schedule; he believes he deserves this because of his service and seniority.   There is now a shortage of nurses. Jorge's supervisor, Marisa, has been trying to hire new nurses, some of whom will only work if they can have Jorge's schedule. Marisa and Jorge are meeting to discuss the situation.

1. What factors are likely to influence the perceptions of Jorge and Marisa?

_____

_____

2. Prepare perception-checking statements for Jorge and Marisa to deliver to one another.

_____

_____

3. How can Marisa and Jorge communicate competently in order to come to a constructive conclusion to this situation?

_____

_____

4.   What suggestions would you give Marisa and Jorge advice based on information in this chapter. Cite information from the text to back up your suggestions.

_____

_____

STUDY GUIDE

Check Your Understanding

CROSSWORD PUZZLE

ACROSS

3. a _____culture values using words to build social harmony rather than to achieve precision

6. the process of attaching meaning to our experiences by selecting, organizing and interpreting

7. compassion for another's situation

10. the ability to project oneself into another person's point of view, so as to experience the other's thoughts and feelings

Class_____   Name _____

11. cognitive frameworks that allow individuals to organize perceptual data that they have selected from the environment
13. perceptual schema that categorize people according to their social positions
14. the process of attaching meaning to behavior

DOWN
1. a _____ culture uses language clearly and logically
2. exaggerating generalizations associated with a categorizing system
3. an effect that illustrates the power of a first impression to influence subsequent perceptions
4. the social and psychological dimensions of men's and women's behavior
5. possessing both masculine and feminine traits
6. gender has a social and a _____ aspect
7. a bias that illustrates the tendency to interpret and explain information in a way that casts oneself in the most favorable manner
8. the process of attaching meaning to events based on their order of occurence
9. perceptual schema that categorize people according to the groups to which they belong
12. a method that involves an examination of the four sides and middle of a perceptual issue

TRUE/FALSE

Mark the statements below as true or false. Correct statements that are false on the lines below to create a true statement.

_____ 1. Androgynous males have a smaller repertoire of behaviors than masculine males.

_____

_____ 2. Selection, organization, interpretation and negotiation comprise the steps of the perception process.

_____

_____ 3. The fact that we pay attention to some things and ignore others illustrates the fact that selection is an objective process.

_____

_____ 4. A perception check is a less threatening way to examine differences of opinions than a direct challenge.

_____

_____ 5. Generalizations and stereotypes of groups are generally accurate for everyone in the group.

_____

_____ 6. The halo effect is the tendency to form an overall positive impression of a person on the basis of one positive characteristic.

_____ 7. Adrenal and sex hormones affect the way both men and women relate to others.

_____

_____ 8. All cultures view talk as desirable, using it for social purposes as well as to perform tasks.

_____

_____ 9. Within the boundaries of a country, most person's perceptions are similar.

_____

_____ 10. The way we perceive ourselves influences our opinions of ourselves, but not our opinions of others.

_____

_____ 11. Since we are able to perceive with our senses, our perceptions make us aware of all that is going on around us.

_____

_____ 12. People with low self-esteem usually have a high opinion of others.

_____

COMPLETION

Fill in the blanks below with the correct terms chosen from the list below.

narrative	self-serving bias	sympathy
punctuation	ethnocentrism	empathy
androgynous	stereotypes	

1. _____ belief that one's culture is superior to others.

2. _____ is the determination of causes and effects in a series of interactions.

3. _____ is a story created by shared perspectives to explain events and behavior.

4. _____ is the tendency to judge ourselves in the most generous terms possible.

5. _____ is the ability to re-create another person's perspective.

6. _____ is feeling compassion for another person.

7. _____ are exaggerated generalizations associated with a categorizing system.

8. _____ is an example of a psychological sex type that influences perception.

MULTIPLE CHOICE

RECOGNIZING PERCEPTION-CHECKING ELEMENTS

For each of the following statements, identify which element of the perception-checking statement is missing. Place the letter of the most accurate evaluation of the statement on the line before the statement.

a. This statement doesn't describe behavior.
b. This statement doesn't give two distinctly different interpretations.
c. This statement doesn't request clarification of the behavior in an open-ended way.
d. There is nothing missing from this perception-checking statement.

_____ 1. "Why did you send me those flowers? Is this a special occasion or what?"

_____ 2. "When you went straight to bed when you came home, I thought you were sick. Are you all right?"

_____ 3. "You must be either really excited about your grades or anxious to talk about something important. What's going on?"

_____ 4. "When you ran out smiling, I figured you were glad to see me and ready to go, or maybe you were having such a good time here you wanted to stay longer."

_____ 5. "I thought you were angry with me when you didn't come over this afternoon like you'd said you would. But then I thought maybe something came up at work. What is it?"

_____ 6. "When you told me you expected to get an outline with my report, I thought you were trying to trick me into doing more work, or maybe you didn't realize that wasn't part of my job."

_____ 7. "When you told everyone my parents own the company, you must have been indicating I was hired here only because of them. Is that what you think?"

_____ 8. "When you passed the ball to me, I thought you wanted me to shoot. Did you?"

_____ 9. "Why is it that you're so pleased with yourself? Did you win the lottery or accomplish something great? What's up?"

_____ 10. "Dad, when you told my friend Art what a great athlete you think I am, I thought you were either really proud of me and wanted to brag a little, or maybe you wanted to see what Art and I had in common by the way he responded. What were your intentions?"

CHAPTER 3 STUDY GUIDE ANSWERS

CROSSWORD PUZZLE

Across:
- 3. high-context
- 6. perception
- 7. sympathy
- 10. empathy
- 11. schema
- 13. roles
- 14. attribution

Down:
- 1. low-context
- 2. stereotyping
- 3. halo
- 4. gender
- 5. androgynous
- 6. psychology
- 7. self-serving
- 8. punctuation
- 9. membership
- 12. pillow

TRUE/FALSE

1. F	4. T	7. T	10. F
2. T	5. F	8. F	11. F
3. F	6. T	9. F	12. F

COMPLETION

1. ethnocentrism
2. punctuation
3. narrative
4. self-serving bias

5. empathy
6. sympathy
7. stereotypes
8. androgynous

MULTIPLE CHOICE

| 1. b | 3. a | 5. d | 7. b, c | 9. a |
| 2. b, c | 4. c | 6. c | 8. b | 10. d |

C H A P T E R   F O U R

Emotions: Thinking, Feeling, and Communicating

OUTLINE

Use this outline to take notes as you read the chapter in the text and/or as your instructor lectures in class.

I.   **COMPONENTS OF EMOTIONS**
   A. **Physiological Factors**
   B. **Nonverbal Reactions**
   C. **Cognitive Interpretations**
   D. **Verbal Expression**

II. **INFLUENCES ON EMOTIONAL EXPRESSION**
   A. **Personality**
   B. **Culture**
   C. **Gender**
   D. **Social Conventions**
   E. **Fear of Self-Disclosure**
   F. **Emotional Contagion**

III. **GUIDELINES FOR EXPRESSING EMOTIONS**
   A. **Recognize Feelings**
   B. **Recognize the Difference between Feeling, Talking and Acting**
   C. **Expand your Emotional Vocabulary**
       1. Avoid emotional counterfeits
          2.   Express verbally
          a.   Use single words
          b.   Describe what's happening to you
          c.   Describe what you'd like to do
       3. Avoid minimizing feelings
       4. Avoid coded feelings
       5. Focus on a specific set of circumstances
   D. **Share Multiple Feelings**
   E. **Consider When and Where to Express your Feelings**

    F. Accept Responsibility for your Feelings
    G. Be Mindful of the Communication Channel

IV. MANAGING DIFFICULT EMOTIONS
    A. Facilitative and Debilitative Emotions
       1. Intensity
       2. Duration
    B. Sources of Debilitative Emotions
       1. Physiology
          a. Genetic makeup
          b. Amygdala's "fight or flight" response
       2. Emotional Memory
       3. Self-talk
          a. rational-emotive theory
          b. rumination

    C. Irrational Thinking and Debilitative Emotions
       1. Fallacy of perfection
       2. Fallacy of approval
       3. Fallacy of shoulds
       4. Fallacy of overgeneralization
          a. Limited amount of evidence
          b. Exaggerated shortcomings
          c. Abuse of the verb "to be"
       5. Fallacy of causation
          a. Belief: you cause emotions in others
          b. Belief: others cause your emotions
       6. Fallacy of helplessness
       7. Fallacy of catastrophic expectations
    D. Minimizing Debilitative Emotions
       1. Monitor your emotional reactions
       2. Note the activating event
       3. Record your self-talk
       4. Dispute your irrational beliefs

KEY TERMS

debilitative emotions	fallacy of causation	
emotional contagion	fallacy of helplessness	rumination
facilitative emotions	fallacy of overgeneralization	self-talk
fallacy of approval	fallacy of perfection	
fallacy of catastrophic expectations	fallacy of shoulds	

ACTIVITIES

4.1 THE COMPONENTS OF EMOTION
Activity Type: Skill Builder/Group Activity

PURPOSE

To identify the components of emotion.

INSTRUCTIONS

1. Read the situations below and describe how the emotions you would experience might manifest themselves in each of the components listed. If you are working in a group, after all have finished, compare the responses of group members.
2. Next record three examples of your own (include the incident, physiological changes, nonverbal reactions, cognitive interpretations, and verbal expressions. If you wish, share one example with the group.

Example

Incident: _____

Physiological changes: _____

Nonverbal reactions: _____

Cognitive interpretations: _____

Verbal expression: _____

1. Incident: Your romantic partner says, "I need to talk to you about something."

Physiological changes: _____

Nonverbal reactions: _____

Cognitive interpretations: _____

Verbal expression: _____

2. Incident: You run into an "ex" while out with a new partner.

Physiological changes: _____

Nonverbal reactions: _____

Cognitive interpretations: _____

Verbal expression: _____

3.   Incident: As you're telling a story, you notice your listener stifle a yawn.

   Physiological changes: _____

   Nonverbal reactions: _____

   Cognitive interpretations: _____

   Verbal expression: _____

4.   Incident: Your professor says, "I'd like to see you in my office after class."

   Physiological changes: _____

   Nonverbal reactions: _____

   Cognitive interpretations: _____

   Verbal expression: _____

YOUR EXAMPLES

1.   Incident: _____

   Physiological changes: _____

   Nonverbal reactions: _____

   Cognitive interpretations: _____

   Verbal expression: _____

2.   Incident: _____

   Physiological changes: _____

   Nonverbal reactions: _____

   Cognitive interpretations: _____

   Verbal expression: _____

3.   Incident: _____

   Physiological changes: _____

   Nonverbal reactions: _____

   Cognitive interpretations: _____

   Verbal expression: _____

4.2 EXPRESS THE FEELINGS
Activity Type: Skill Builder

PURPOSES

1. To distinguish true feeling statements from counterfeit expressions of emotion.
2. To increase your ability to express your feelings clearly.

INSTRUCTIONS

1. Analyze the statements below to determine which of the seven guidelines for expressing emotions are followed or ignored. There may be more than one.

   1.   Recognize Feelings
   2.   Recognize the Difference between Feeling, Talking and Acting
   3.   Expand your Emotional Vocabulary
         A. Avoid emotional counterfeits
         B. Express verbally
              a.   Use single words
              b.   Describe what's happening to you
              c.   Describe what you'd like to do
         C.   Avoid minimizing feelings
         D.   Avoid coded feelings
         E.   Focus on a specific set of circumstances
   4.   Share Multiple Feelings
   5.   Consider When and Where to Express your Feelings
   6.   Accept Responsibility for your Feelings
   7.   Be Mindful of the Communication Channel

2. Rewrite statements that do not follow the above guidelines to clearly or accurately express the speaker's feelings
3. Record examples of your own at the end of the exercise.

EXAMPLE

That's the most disgusting thing I've ever heard!

Analysis: *This isn't a satisfactory statement, since the speaker isn't clearly claiming that he or she is disgusted. The speaker doesn't seem to recognize feelings (1) and doesn't verbally express a feeling(3-B) and doesn't accept responsibility by using "I" language (6).*

Restatement: *I'm upset and angry that those parents left their young children alone overnight.*

1. You're being awfully sensitive about that.

   Analysis _____

   Restatement _____

   _____

2. I can't figure out how to approach him.

   Analysis _____

   Restatement _____

_____

3. I'm confused about what you want from me.

    Analysis _____

    Restatement _____

    _____

4. I feel as if you're trying to hurt me.

    Analysis _____

    Restatement _____

    _____

5. You make me so mad when you're late.

    Analysis _____

    Restatement _____

    _____

6. I'm sort of upset with your behavior and a little bit annoyed that you don't apologize.

    Analysis _____

    Restatement _____

    _____

7. I see you're all in there enjoying the game while I clean up the kitchen.

    Analysis _____

    Restatement _____

    _____

8. I feel like the rug's been pulled out from under me.

    Analysis _____

    Restatement _____

    _____

Now record three feeling statements of your own. Analyze and, if necessary, restate.

1. _____.

    Analysis _____

Restatement _____

_____

2.   _____.

Analysis _____

Restatement _____

_____

3.   _____.

Analysis _____

Restatement _____

_____

FEEDBACK TO "4.2 EXPRESS THE FEELINGS"

1. Guidelines 1 and 3-B are not followed. The speaker here is labeling another's feelings, but saying nothing about his or her own feelings. Is the speaker concerned, irritated, or indifferent? We don't know. Possible restate: "I worried that I teased you too much about your hair."

2. Guidelines 1 and 3-B are not followed. The emotion here is implied but not stated. The speaker might be frustrated, perplexed, or tired. Possible restate: "I'm nervous about telling him why I was absent."

3. Here is a clear statement of the speaker's emotional state.

4. Guideline 3-A isn't followed; it is emotionally counterfeit. Just because we say "I feel" doesn't mean a feeling is being expressed. This is an interpretation statement because "I feel" can be replaced by "I think". The speaker is expressing that "I think you tried to hurt me" and could then go on to state "I'm anxious about trusting you after you lied to me last week."

5. Guideline 6 is not followed; the speaker doesn't accept responsibility but blames the other person. Possibly there are multiple feelings, guideline 4. Possible restate: "I feel frustrated, hurt and angry when you're late.

6. Guideline 3-C isn't followed; it is minimizing with words like "sort of" "a bit." Possible restate: "I'm upset with your behavior and annoyed that you don't apologize."

7. Probably guideline 3-D isn't followed and it is coded. Possible restate: "I feel used and taken for granted and would like some help cleaning up so we can all watch the game."

8. Here's a metaphorical statement of feeling, strongly suggesting surprise or shock. This sort of message probably does an adequate job of expressing the emotion here, but it might be too vague for some people to understand. Possible restate: "I feel insecure right now since I didn't get the job I was expecting."

4.3 STATING EMOTIONS EFFECTIVELY

Activity Type: Skill Builder

PURPOSE

To help you express the emotions you experience clearly and appropriately.

INSTRUCTIONS

1.   Identify what's ineffective or unclear about each of the following feeling statements.
2.   Rewrite the feeling statements making them more effective using the guidelines from your text:
    1.   Recognize Feelings
    2.   Recognize the Difference between Feeling, Talking and Acting
    3.   Expand your Emotional Vocabulary
        A. Avoid emotional counterfeits
        B. Express verbally
            a.   Use single words
            b.   Describe what's happening to you
            c.   Describe what you'd like to do
        C. Avoid minimizing feelings
        D. Avoid coded feelings
        E. Focus on a specific set of circumstances
    4.   Share Multiple Feelings
    5.   Consider When and Where to Express your Feelings
    6.   Accept Responsibility for your Feelings
    7.   Be Mindful of the Communication Channel

FEELING STATEMENT	IDENTIFY INEFFECTIVE, UNCLEAR ELEMENTS/REWRITE STATEMENT
EXAMPLE *When you complimented me in front of everyone at the party, I was really embarrassed.*	*I didn't express the mixed emotions I was feeling. I could have expressed this better by saying, "When you complimented me last night at the party, I was glad you were proud of me, but I was embarrassed that so many people heard it."*
1. You should be more sensitive.	
2. I get kind of jealous when you have lunch with colleagues.	
3. I don't hear anyone offering to help with this project.	

4. Well, I guess you don't really care about this – or me.	
5. When you act like that, I don't want to be seen with you.	

FEELING STATEMENT	IDENTIFY INEFFECTIVE, UNCLEAR ELEMENTS/REWRITE STATEMENT
6. You make me happy.	
7. Why should I help you now? You never show me any appreciation.	
8. I was a little ticked off when you didn't show up.	
9. You jerk—you forgot to put gas in the car!	
10. It's about time you paid up.	
11. I guess I'm a little attracted to him.	
12. With all that's happened, I feel like I'm in a time warp.	

4.4 SELF-TALK

Activity Type: Skill Builder/Group Activity

PURPOSES

1. To discover the self-talk in many common statements.
2. To identify fallacies in self-talk.
3. To dispute irrational self-talk.

INSTRUCTIONS

1. In groups, analyze the statements below.
2. Expand the self-talk behind each statement by using details from your experience to help discover things people often say to themselves.
3. Identify any fallacies contained in the self-talk: approval, overgeneralization, perfection, helplessness, shoulds, catastrophic expectations, causation
4. Dispute any irrational self-talk.
5. As a group, record the most common examples of your own self-talk, the fallacies involved, and the disputing you need to do to keep emotionally healthy.

STATEMENT	SELF-TALK	FALLACIES	DISPUTE ANY FALLACIES
Example: She's so critical.	She never has anything good to say. She drives me crazy. I can't stand her. I'll never be able to make her happy.	Overgeneralization, Causation, Helplessness, Approval	I need to focus on the good things she does say, not the criticisms. She doesn't make me crazy; I let her get to me. If I don't like what she is saying at the moment, I can leave. It would be nice to please her, but I don't need her approval to be happy.
1. No one appreciates me around here.			
2. He's so moody.			

STATEMENT	SELF-TALK	FALLACIES	DISPUTE ANY FALLACIES
3. I don't know why I even bother to study for her stupid tests.			
4. Why can't he be more sensitive to my feelings?			
5. She is so embarrassing because she has no manners.			
6. He's a jerk just like his brother.			
7. She's the perfect boss. I'll be completely satisfied in this job.			
8. I'll never get out of here with all her talking.			

	SELF-TALK	FALLACIES	DISPUTE ANY FALLACIES
9. I can't believe you told me to buy this worthless car.			
10. It's no use talking to him; he's so unreasonable.			
YOUR OWN EXAMPLES: **STATEMENT**	**SELF-TALK**	**FALLACIES**	**DISPUTE ANY FALLACIES**
1.			
2.			
3.			
4.			

4.5 DISPUTING IRRATIONAL THOUGHTS

Activity Type: Invitation to Insight

PURPOSE

To help you minimize debilitative emotions by eliminating irrational thinking.

INSTRUCTIONS

1. Use the chart provided to record activating events in which you experience **communication-related** debilitative emotions. The events needn't involve overwhelming, intense or intimae feelings; consider mildly debilitative emotions as well.
2. For each incident (activating event), record the self-talk that leads to the emotion you experienced.
3. If the self-talk you've identified is based on any of the irrational fallacies described in *Looking Out/Looking In*, identify them.
4. In each case where irrational thinking exists, dispute the irrational fallacies and provide an alternative, more rational interpretation of the event.
5. After completing the examples, record your conclusions here (or put them on a separate page):

CONCLUSIONS

1. What are the situations in which you often experience debilitative emotions?

    _____

    _____

2. What irrational beliefs do you subscribe to most often? Label them and explain.

    _____

    _____

    _____

3. How can you think more rationally to reduce the number and intensity of debilitative emotions? (Give specific examples related to other aspects of your life, as well as referring to the activating events you have described in this exercise.)

    _____

    _____

    _____

    _____

ACTIVATING EVENT	SELF-TALK	IRRATIONAL FALLACIES	EMOTION(S)	DISPUTE FALLACIES AND PROVIDE ALTERNATE RATIONAL THINKING
Example: *Getting ready for job interview*	*The employer will ask me questions I can't answer. I'll mess up for sure. I'll never get a good job — it's hopeless!*	*catastrophic failure overgeneralization helplessness*	*apprehension despair*	*I've prepared for the questions and the interview, so if I'm asked something I don't know, I'll say I'll get back to them on that. I have interpersonal skills. I'll find a good job with time and effort.*
1.				
2.				
3.				
4.				

5.

4.6 MEDIATED MESSAGES – EXPRESSING EMOTION

Activity Type: Group Discussion

PURPOSE

To evaluate the expression of emotion in mediated contexts.

INSTRUCTIONS

Discuss each of the questions below in your group. Prepare written answers for your instructor, or be prepared to contribute to a large group discussion, comparing your experiences with those of others in your class.

1. Describe how to recognize emotions communicated in mediated channels such as post-it notes, e-mail, and instant messaging.

   _____

   _____

2. Emotional expression may be more difficult in a mediated context (e.g., lack of touch or facial expression to communicate your empathy). On the other hand, mediated contexts may make emotional expression easier (e.g., write a note upon the death of someone rather than face them). Cite examples from your life where you used mediated contexts to express emotion.

   _____

   _____

   _____

   _____

3. In written communication, some stylistic devices (underlining, exclamation marks, capital letters, emoticons like the smiley, winking or sad face) indicate emotion. How effective do you think these can be in expressing emotion? How easily and how often are they understood? Misunderstood?

   _____

   _____

   _____

4. Compare and contrast the effectiveness of voice-messages and text-messages for conveying emotion through words.

   _____

   _____

_____

_____

4.7 YOUR CALL – EXPRESSING EMOTION
Activity Type: Group Discussion

PURPOSE

To evaluate the expression of emotion in an applied context.

INSTRUCTIONS

Use the case below and the discussion questions that follow to discuss the variety of communication issues involved in effective communication. Make notes on this page, add other pages on your own, or prepare a group report/analysis based on your discussion. Add your own experiences to individualize the analysis to make it *Your* Call.

CASE

Marcos and Alessandra have been dating for over a year. They love each other and are considering marriage, but each has at least one big reservation about the other. Marcos thinks Alessandra is moody; it seems that one minute she is "up" and happy with everyone, including him, and the next she is feeling crabby and criticizes everything about him. Alessandra finds Marcos difficult because he seems to keep everything inside; she wants him to tell her when he feels good and bad in detail, but he says nothing or responds with only a few words.

1. What is the appropriate level of emotional expression between dating partners? Do you think either Marcos or Alessandra should change the way they express their emotions?

_____

_____

2. Do you think Marcos and Alessandra perceive the emotional climate of the other accurately? Are there any influences on emotional expression that might exist here (personality, culture, gender, social conventions, fear of self-disclosure , or emotional contagion)?

_____

_____

3. Can you identify any irrational fallacies (approval, overgeneralization, perfection, helplessness, shoulds, catastrophic expectations, causation) in either Marcos or Alessandra that might trigger debilitative emotions?

_____

_____

4. What would you recommend that would help Marcos and Alessandra more effectively express their emotions?

_____

_____

STUDY GUIDE

CHECK YOUR UNDERSTANDING

CROSSWORD PUZZLE

ACROSS

5. changes that are the body's internal physical response to strong emotions
8. emotions that prevent a person from functioning effectively
13. a fallacy of thinking that believes that no errors should be made in communication performance

DOWN

1. interpretation or thought that accompanies strong emotions
2. reactions that are the visible physical signs in response to strong emotions
3. emotions that are combinations of emotions

4. emotions that contribute to effective functioning
6. basic emotions
7. the nonvocal process of thinking
9. the strength of an emotion
10. the fallacy of thinking that believes that acceptance is needed from others
11. a powerful form of debilitative self-talk in which the person dwells on negative thoughts
 12. the length of an emotion

TRUE/FALSE

Mark the statements below as true or false. Correct statements that are false on the lines below to create a true statement.

      1. Marriage researcher John Gottman found that when couples are in such intense conflict that bodily changes occur (increased heart rate, a rise in blood pressure, a dilation of pupils) effective problem-solving is impeded.

_____

_____ 2. Although "primary" emotions may vary from culture to culture, most scholars acknowledge that *anger*, *joy*, *fear*, and *sadness* are common and typical human emotions.

_____

_____ 3. While expression of emotion varies with culture and gender, scholars find that around the world both men and women consistently and similarly speak the phrase "I love you."

_____

_____ 4. In mainstream North American society, the unwritten rules of communication encourage the direct expression of most emotion.

_____

_____ 5. "I feel confined" is an emotional counterfeit statement.

_____

_____ 6. Using many words to express a feeling is better than just summarizing feelings in a few words.

_____

_____ 7. Anger (or any other emotions) can be debilitative or facilitative, depending on the intensity and duration.

_____

_____ 8. Outgoing people report more negative emotions in everyday life than do those who are less social.

_____

_____ 9. Subscribing to the myth of perfection usually enhances your own self-esteem, but it usually doesn't keep others from liking you.

_____

_____ 10. The fallacy of causation exists in two forms: you believe others cause your emotions or you believe you cause others' emotions.

_____

COMPLETION

Fill in the blanks below with the correct terms chosen from the list below.

catastrophic expectations	helplessness	causation
overgeneralization	shoulds	approval
perfection	activating event	monitoring
disputing		

1. _____ is an irrational fallacy that operates on the assumption that if something bad can possibly happen, it will.

2. _____ is an irrational fallacy that suggests that satisfaction in life is determined by forces beyond your control.

3. _____ is an irrational fallacy based on the belief that emotions are the result of other people and things rather than one's own self-talk.

4. _____ is an irrational fallacy that makes a broad claim based on a limited amount of evidence.

5. _____ is an irrational fallacy based on the inability to distinguish between what is and what ought to be.

6. _____ is an irrational fallacy in which people go to incredible lengths to seek acceptance from virtually everyone.

7. _____ is an irrational fallacy in which people believe that worthwhile communicators should be able to handle every situation with complete confidence and skill.

8. _____ is the single large incident or series of small incidents that lead to thoughts or beliefs about the incident.

9. _____ is the process of recognizing the physiological, nonverbal, and cognitive components of emotions.

10. _____ is the process of recognizing mistaken thinking and developing alternative thinking.

MULTIPLE CHOICE

Choose the letter of the irrational fallacy contained in the self-talk found below.

a. perfection   e. causation
b. approval   f. helplessness
c. shoulds   g. catastrophic expectations
d. overgeneralization

_____ 1. "If only I didn't put my foot in my mouth when I ask someone out."

_____ 2. "I just can't initiate conversations—that's all there is to it."

_____ 3. "He shouldn't be off with his friends on Friday night."

_____ 4. "If she doesn't like this shirt, I'll be so upset."

_____ 5. "There was a major fire the last time we left; there will probably be an earthquake this time."

_____ 6. "He's never romantic."

_____ 7. "She's always a cold fish; I'm lucky if I get a kiss."

_____ 8. "Other people ought to cut me some slack; they shouldn't be so critical."

_____ 9. "You're going to die or be seriously injured if you go to Mexico at spring break."

_____ 10. "I've had a class in interpersonal communication; I can't believe I insulted her just now."

_____ 11. "Shaw makes me so mad with all his great grades."

_____ 12. "She'll be devastated if I break up with her."

_____ 13. "It's not even worth trying to reach him."

_____ 14. "I hope they don't notice how much weight I've gained. They won't like it."

Choose the best answer for each of the statements below.

15. Which of the following statements about emotions and culture is true?

    a. The same events will generate the same emotions in all cultures.
    b. Some emotions seem to be experienced by people around the world.
    c. People from different cultures express happiness and sadness with different facial expressions.
    d. Fear of strangers is as strong in Japan as it is in the U.S.

16. Which of the following statements about gender and emotion is true?

    a. Women and men are equally likely to express feelings of vulnerability.
    b. Men and women are equally good at recognizing the emotions of others.
    c. Men are less bashful about revealing their strengths and positive emotions than women are.
    d. Women are less likely than men to recognize others' emotions.

17. Which of these represents coded emotions?

    a. I feel grateful when you bring soup to me when I'm sick.
    b. I'm upset because you borrowed my white-out.

    c.   I feel like a door mat—just used by everyone.

    d.   I don't hear any thank-you's. It sure would be nice to hear some appreciation.

18. Which of the following follows the text's guidelines for expressing feelings?

    a.   "I feel like watching a movie."
    b.   "I feel like you're lonely."
    c.   "I'm irritated by the ticking clock."
    d.   "I'm totally involved."

19. Which of the following *best* improves the expression of emotion in the statement "I feel like giving up"?

    a.   "I'm frustrated after asking him to pay his telephone bill three times."
    b.   "I'm going to kill him."
    c.   "I am going to tell the landlord about this frustrating situation."
    d.   "I feel he's been unreasonable."

20.   The biological structure in the brain that scans our experiences for threats is called the:
    a.   sentinel
    b.   neurotransmitter
    c.   synapsis
    d.   amygdala

CHAPTER 4 STUDY GUIDE ANSWERS

CROSSWORD PUZZLE

Across
- 5. physiological
- 8. debilitative
- 11. perfection

Down
- 1. cognitive
- 2. nonverbal
- 3. mixed
- 4. facilitative
- 6. primary
- 7. self-talk
- 9. intensity
- 10. approval
- 12. duration
- 13. rumination

TRUE/FALSE

1. T	3. F	5. F	7. T	9. F
2. T	4. F	6. F	8. F	10. T

COMPLETION

1. catastrophic expectations
2. helplessness
3. causation
4. overgeneralization
5. shoulds
6. approval
7. perfection
8. activating event
9. monitoring
10. disputing

MULTIPLE CHOICE

1. a	5. g	9. g	13. f	17. d
2. f	6. d	10. a	14. b	18. c
3. c	7. d	11. e	15. b	19. a
4. b	8. c	12. e	16. c	20. d

C H A P T E R   F I V E

Language: Barrier and Bridge

OUTLINE

Use this outline to take notes as you read the chapter in the text and/or as your instructor lectures in class.

I. LANGUAGE IS SYMBOLIC
    A. signs
    B. symbols

II. UNDERSTANDINGS AND MISUNDERSTANDINGS
    A. Understanding Words: Semantic Rules
        1. Equivocation
        2. Relative language
        3. Static evaluation
        4. Abstraction vs. behavioral language
           a.   advantages
           b.   problems

    B. Understanding Structure: Syntactic Rules
        1. Grammar
        2. Order
    C. Understanding Context: Pragmatic Rules
        1. Often unstated
        2. Relies on coordination
        3. Personal codes

III. THE IMPACT OF LANGUAGE
    A. Naming and Identity
        1. Connotations
        2. Personal identity
        3. Group identity

    B. Affiliation
        1. Convergence
        2. Divergence

    C. Power
        1. Powerless speech mannerism

2. Culture and context

D. Disruptive Language
1. Fact-opinion confusion
2. Fact-inference confusion
3. Emotive language

E. The Language of Responsibility
1. "It" statements
2. "But" statements
3. Questions vs. statements
4. "I" and "You" language

   a. "You" language judges
   b. "I" statements describe
      1) other's behavior
      2) your interpretation
      3) your feelings
      4) consequences of the behavior
   c. Advantages of "I" language
      1) Accepts responsibility
      2) Reduces defensiveness
      3) Is more accurate
   d. Reservations about "I" language
      1) Anger impedes use
      2) Defensiveness with poor nonverbal
      3) Sounds artificial without confidence
      4) Too much sounds narcissistic

5. "We" language
      1) May signal inclusion and commitment
      2) May speak improperly for others
      3) Consider combining "I" and "we"

III. GENDER AND LANGUAGE
A. Content
1. Some common topics
2. Sex talk restricted to same gender
3. Many topics vary by gender

B. Reasons for Communicating
1. build and maintain social relationships
   a. Men: more joking and good-natured teasing
   b. Women: more feelings and relationships
2. Women—nourish relationships, build harmony
3. Men – task-oriented, advice, status, independence

C. Conversational Style
1. Men: judge, direct, and "I" language
2. Women: questions, intensifiers, emotion, uncertainty, support, maintain conversations

D. Nongender Variables

      1. Occupation & Social philosophy
      2. Historical and gender roles

V. CULTURE AND LANGUAGE
A. Verbal Communication Styles
      1. Direct/indirect (low-context and high-context cultures)
      2. Elaborate/succinct
      3. Formality/informality
B. Language and World View
      1. Linguistic relativism
      2. Sapir-Whorf hypothesis

KEY TERMS

abstraction ladder	linguistic relativism
abstract language	low-context cultures
behavioral language	powerless speech mannerisms
"but" statements	pragmatic rules
convergence	relative words
divergence	Sapir-Whorf hypothesis
emotive language	semantic rules
equivocal language	static evaluation
high-context cultures	syntactic rules
"I" language	"we" language
"it" statements	"you" language

ACTIVITIES

5.1 MISUNDERSTOOD LANGUAGE

Activity Type: Skill Builder

PURPOSE

To recognize and change language that contributes to misunderstanding.

INSTRUCTIONS

1. Label the language contained in each of the sentences below as relative language, static evaluation, or equivocal language. See pages 159-162.
2. Rewrite each sentence in more precise language.
3. Write your own examples of each variety of language in the spaces provided.

EXAMPLE 1

I'm trying to diet, so give me a **small** piece of cake.

Language *Relative language*

Why you categorized it as you did and how can you best correct it: *It is relative because it can be compared to many other things; the best way to correct it is to use a number.*

Revised statement *I'm trying to diet, so give me a piece of cake about two inches square.*

EXAMPLE 2

Helen **is** a troublemaker.

Language *Static evaluation*

Why you categorized it as you did and how can you best correct it: *It is static because it uses the verb "to be" implying that troublemaker is a permanent condition of Helen. It can best be corrected with behavioral description.*

Revised statement *Helen told my mother that I was out until 3 a.m. with Jim.*

EXAMPLE 3

There's a new book in the library; you should **check it out.**

Language *Equivocal language*

 Why you categorized it as you did and how can you best correct it: *It is equivocal because "check it out" can mean to appropriately remove it from the library in your name or to peruse it. Correct it by clarifying the meaning.*

Revised statement *There's a new book in the library; you should peruse it and see if it is something you'd like to read.*

1. What do you want to know about **our relationship?**

    Language _____

    Why you categorized it as you did and how can you best correct it: _____

    _____

    Revised statement _____

    _____

2. They **are** real nerds.

   Language _____

   Why you categorized it as you did and how can you best correct it: _____

   _____

   Revised statement _____

   _____

3. She's very **conservative**.

   Language _____

   Why you categorized it as you did and how can you best correct it: _____

   _____

   Revised statement _____

   _____

4. I haven't done my laundry for a **long time**.

   Language _____

   Why you categorized it as you did and how can you best correct it: _____

   _____

   Revised statement _____

   _____

5. Your essay should be **brief**.

   Language _____

   Why you categorized it as you did and how can you best correct it: _____

   _____

   Revised statement _____

   _____

6. My job isn't **taking me anywhere**.

   Language _____

   Why you categorized it as you did and how can you best correct it: _____

   _____

Revised statement _____

_____

_____

7. She **is** such a braggart.

Language _____

Revised statement _____

_____

8. You've got especially **poor attendance**.

Language _____

Why you categorized it as you did and how can you best correct it: _____

_____

Revised statement _____

_____

Now write your own examples of each type of language and revise the statements to illustrate alternative language.

1. Equivocal language _____

_____

Revised _____

_____

2. Relative language _____

_____

Revised _____

_____

3. Static evaluation _____

_____

Revised _____

_____

5.2 BEHAVIORAL LANGUAGE

Activity Type: Skill Builder

PURPOSE

To increase the clarity of your language by using behavioral descriptions.

INSTRUCTIONS

In each of the situations below, change the language to describe behavior in specific terms. Remember to focus on the <u>behavior</u> (e.g., Bev <u>did</u> "x," rather than Bev <u>is</u> "x"). If you are giving instructions, be specific enough (low abstractions) to clearly get your idea across to someone else. See pages 161-163.

EXAMPLE 1

John's a live wire.

John ran a 5K in the morning, volunteered for two hours at the homeless shelter in the afternoon, and then danced at a party until dawn.

EXAMPLE 2

Go over that way.

Go across the footbridge, turn right, go up the five large steps to the third building on your left.

1.   Will you just wash the car the right way this time?

_____

_____

2.   Natasha needs to get real.

_____

_____

3.   You can't rely on Randy.

_____

_____

4.   That teacher is hard-headed.

_____

_____

5.   Get organized.

_____

_____

6.   Josh just blows me off when I have something important to say.

_____

_____

7. He acts weird.

_____

_____

9. Do the report correctly this time.

_____

_____

10. My parents are understanding.

_____

_____

11. Get a decent movie this time.

_____

_____

12. I like it that your family is emotional.

_____

_____

5.3 RESPONSIBLE LANGUAGE

Activity Type: Skill Builder

PURPOSE

To rewrite evaluative statements into descriptive ones.

INSTRUCTIONS

1. Rewrite each evaluative "you" statement into descriptive "I" language. See pages 161-163 and 175-180.

   Use all four elements of the complete "I" statement:
   a. Describe the other person's behavior
   b. Give your interpretation of the behavior
   c. Identify your feelings
   d. Give the consequences that the other person's behavior has for you.

   Be careful to
   a. Use specific, low level abstractions
   b. Take responsibility for your thoughts and feelings (don't say, "I feel you're . . .")
   c. Avoid loaded terms like "you wouldn't <u>even</u>", "you could <u>at least</u>," finally, whenever, ever since, always, "I can't believe that," "Just because," "When you kept on," etc.

2. Record examples of your own at the end and rewrite them.

EXAMPLE 1
"You don't care about my feelings."
> *Behavior: I saw you in the coffee shop with your old girlfriend when you told me you had to work.*
> *Interpretation: I thought you lied to me about where you were going.*
> *Feeling: I'm hurt and confused.*
> *Consequence: I'm not sure of where we stand in our relationship.*

EXAMPLE 2
"That was a dumb move!"
> *Behavior: You used the high setting to dry my favorite cotton shirt.*
> *Interpretation: I figured you were in a rush and forgot it needed a lower setting.*
> *Feeling: I'm irritated*
> *Consequence: because it doesn't fit me now.*

1. "You messed up my whole semester."

   Behavior _____

   Interpretation_____

   Feeling _____

   Consequence _____

2. "You're such a drama queen."

   Behavior _____

Interpretation_____

Feeling _____

Consequence _____

3. "You can't be trusted."

Behavior _____

Interpretation_____

Feeling _____

Consequence _____

4. "Stop trying to control my life."

Behavior _____

Interpretation_____

Feeling _____

Consequence _____

5. "You don't trust me ever."

Behavior _____

Interpretation_____

Feeling _____

Consequence _____

6. "You're so full of yourself."

Behavior _____

Interpretation_____

Feeling _____

Consequence _____

7. "You make me doubt our relationship."

Behavior _____

Interpretation_____

Feeling _____

Consequence _____

8. "You have a bad attitude."

Behavior _____

Interpretation_____

Feeling _____

Consequence _____

9. "You're never there for me."

Behavior _____

Interpretation_____

Feeling _____

Consequence _____

10. "You're not really trying to get a job."

Behavior _____

Interpretation_____

Feeling _____

Consequence _____

Record your own "you" language statements here. Rewrite them using "I" language.

11. _____.

Behavior _____

Interpretation_____

Feeling _____

Consequence _____

12. _____.

Behavior _____

Interpretation_____

Feeling _____

Consequence _____

5.4 "I" LANGUAGE

Activity Type: Oral Skill

PURPOSE

To evaluate your skill in delivering "I" language statements.

INSTRUCTIONS

1. Form partners. Identify situations in your lives in which both "you" and "I" language messages might be delivered. See pages 175-180.
2. Deliver in a realistic manner both a "you" message and an "I" message to your partner according to Chapter 5 of *Looking Out/Looking In* and outlined in the checklist below.
3. Describe on a separate sheet of paper
   a. how well "I" language might (or might not) work in the situation you have chosen. If you do not think "I" language is the best approach for this situation, explain why and describe a more promising alternative.
   b. the degree to which you could (or could not) increase your communicative competence by using "I" language in other situations.

CHECKLIST 1

_____   Delivers a "you" message to partner.

_____   Delivers the same message in "I" language, without using notes

      _____   Describes the other's specific behavior(s) in specific, behavioral terms, using non-evaluative language

      _____ Describes your interpretation of the behavior

      _____   Describes your feelings arising from other's behavior(s).

      _____   Describes consequences of other's behavior(s) as appropriate for self, for the other person, for third parties, or for the relationship.

_____   Verbal and nonverbal behavior

      _____   Reflects responsibility for "owning" the message.

      _____   Sounds realistic and consistent with personal style.

            _____ Avoids creating defensive climate

_____   Evaluates probably outcome of "I" message, explaining how it might be used or adapted in this and other real-life situations.

5.4 "I" LANGUAGE (CONTINUED)

CHECKLIST 2

_____   Delivers a "you" message to partner.

_____   Delivers the same message in "I" language, without using notes

      _____   Describes the other's specific behavior(s) in specific, behavioral terms, using non-evaluative language

      _____ Describes your interpretation of the behavior

      _____   Describes your feelings arising from other's behavior(s).

      _____   Describes consequences of other's behavior(s) as appropriate for self, for the other person, for third parties, or for the relationship.

_____   Verbal and nonverbal behavior

      _____   Reflects responsibility for "owning" the message.

      _____   Sounds realistic and consistent with personal style.

            _____ Avoids creating defensive climate

_____   Evaluates probably outcome of "I" message, explaining how it might be used or adapted in this and other real-life situations.

5.5 EFFECTIVE LANGUAGE
Activity Type: Invitation to Insight

PURPOSE

To analyze the types of language you use and the effectiveness of each.

INSTRUCTIONS

1. For each of the situations below, record the type of language used by the speaker. Evaluate its effectiveness. If you cannot identify with the situation, substitute one of your own.
2. Record the language you would use in response. Again, record your own situation and language if you have a relevant one.
3. Label the type of language used and evaluate its effectiveness. Focus on high and low abstraction, powerful or powerless speech mannerisms, facts or opinions, inferences, high- and low-context language styles and language and worldview.
4. Describe any alternative language you could use and its relative effectiveness.

EXAMPLE

Situation: Your supervisor at work has called you aside three times this week to correct work you have done. Each time she says, "You've messed up on this."

Type of language used with you/effectiveness: *My supervisor used "**you**" language and **high abstraction**. It wasn't very effective with me because I wasn't sure exactly what I'd messed up on, and I got very defensive, thinking she was about to fire me. She was very direct with me, however; she didn't keep silent about what was bothering her (this is consistent with the **low-context culture** in which I live).*

Language you'd use in response: *"You're on me all the time about something or other."*

Type of language and effectiveness: *"**You**" language and **high abstraction**. This is probably not very effective. My supervisor is likely to get defensive. Actually, my supervisor may think this is "helpful" and "caring" behavior and not realize that I am feeling hassled and threatened.*

Alternative language: *"Ms. Gomez, I'm worried that I'm not doing my job correctly because you've corrected me three times this week. Which part of the report do you want corrected?." This "I" language is more likely to let Ms. Gomez know what specifically is bothering me without raising a good deal of defensiveness. She's likely to appreciate my directness and specific request for help.*

1. Situation: Your romantic partner has been extremely busy with school and work the last two weeks, and you've been feeling left out. When you suggest going out to a party, your partner replies, "You need a personal circus to have fun."

   Type of language used with you/effectiveness:

   _____

   _____

   Language you'd use in response:

   _____

   _____

   Type of language and effectiveness:

   _____

   _____

Alternative language:

_____

_____

2. Situation: You have a hard time saying "no." Lately your roommate has been asking you to do chores that are not your responsibility. Tonight the roommate says, "You're such a great roommate. You won't mind doing the dishes for me tonight since I've got a date and you're just staying home anyway, will you?"

    Type of language used with you/effectiveness:

    _____

    _____

    Language you'd use in response:

    _____

    _____

    Type of language and effectiveness:

    _____

    _____

    Alternative language:

    _____

    _____

3. Situation: Cousins of yours are moving to town. They just called, addressing you by your old family nickname and said, "You lucky person, you get to have the pleasure of our company for a while until we find a place to live. We thought you'd be glad to have us."

    Type of language used with you/effectiveness:

    _____

    _____

    Language you'd use in response:

    _____

    _____

    Type of language and effectiveness:

_____

_____

Alternative language:

_____

_____

4. Situation: You're working on a project with a partner from class, and the partner says, "We'll never get this done. You're too meticulous about everything."

Type of language used with you/effectiveness:

_____

_____

Language you'd use in response:

_____

_____

Type of language and effectiveness:

_____

_____

Alternative language:

_____

_____

5. Situation: Your boss's five-year-old is visiting the workplace. The child has broken two items and is now running from door to door, laughing loudly. Two customers look your way. Your boss says, "Isn't he great? Really an energetic kid!"

Type of language used with you/effectiveness:

_____

_____

Language you'd use:

_____

_____

Type of language and effectiveness:

_____

_____

Alternative language:

_____

_____

Record a situation of your own here:

6. Situation:

Type of language used with you/effectiveness:

_____

_____

Language you'd use in response:

_____

_____

Type of language and effectiveness:

_____

_____

Alternative language:

_____

_____

5.6 MEDIATED MESSAGES--LANGUAGE
Activity Type: Group Discussion

PURPOSE

To analyze the use of language in mediated contexts.

INSTRUCTIONS

Discuss each of the questions below in your group. Prepare written answers for your instructor, or be prepared to contribute to a large group discussion, comparing your experiences with those of others in your class.

1. Our identity is tied to the names we use. Discuss your identity goals with the name(s) you use in mediated contexts (e.g., *your e-mail address, web site identities or your chat room identity*).

    _____

    _____

    _____

2. The language used in an answering machine, voice mail, or e-mail can be very businesslike or very informal. Discuss the pros and cons of formal versus informal mediated messages.

    _____

    _____

    _____

3. Sometimes people fail to adapt their language style to the medium they are using (e.g., *they leave a 5-minute voice mail that should have been summarized in 30 seconds*). Should different mediated channels contain more language or less? Specify two different mediated channels and how much language is appropriate for each.

    _____

    _____

    _____

4. Describe the gender or social role differences you have noticed in the <u>language</u> of mediated communication. (Example: *My son is more comfortable "talking" about emotions in e-mail, my daughter prefers the telephone.* Example: *My spouse's executive assistant uses very informal language to address me in an e-mail that is never used with me face-to-face.*)

    _____

    _____

    _____

    _____

5.7 YOUR CALL – LANGUAGE
Activity Type: Group Discussion

PURPOSE

To analyze language choices and their effect on a relationship.

INSTRUCTIONS

Use the case below and the discussion questions that follow to discuss the variety of communication issues involved in effective communication. Make notes on this page, add other pages on your own, or prepare a group report/analysis based on your discussion. Add your own experiences to individualize the analysis to make it **Your Call**.

CASE

Professor Polle paired Matt and Magda as class project partners. After three weeks both Matt and Magda came to their professor to complain about the other. Matt called Magda a "flake" and said she didn't work hard enough and didn't take the project seriously. Magda said that Matt was "arrogant," wanted the project done only her way, and didn't care about all the commitments Magda had. It was too late in the semester for the professor to give them new partners.

1. Identify the language that Matt and Magda are using about one another. What effect does using this language have on their perception of each other? On the successful completion of their project?

_____

_____

2. Rewrite the high level abstractions that Matt and Magda use with specific, concrete language. How could this change their perceptions? Improve their situation?

_____

_____

3. Give an example of an "I" language statement from any of the three persons that could improve the situation.

_____

_____

4. Gender and culture may influence the way language is used. Identify differences mentioned in your text and describe how those differences might apply to this situation.

_____

_____

STUDY GUIDE

CHECK YOUR UNDERSTANDING

CROSSWORD PUZZLE

ACROSS

2. language that conveys the sender's attitude rather than simply offering an objective description
5. the use of general terms rather than specific language
8. the process of adapting one's speaking style to match that of others
10. a linguistic device that shows the transitory nature of many objects and behaviors

DOWN

1. language terms that gain their meaning from comparison
2. language that conveys the sender's attitude rather than simply offering an objective description
3. cultures that use language primarily to express thoughts, feelings, and ideas as clearly and logically as possible
6. a language account that refers only to observable phenomena
7. speaking in a way that emphasizes differences from others
9. rules of language that govern the ways symbols can be arranged, as opposed to the meanings of those symbols
11. rules that govern what meaning language has, as opposed to what structure it has
12. a moderate linguistic theory that argues that language exerts a strong influence on the perceptions of the people who speak it
13. rules that govern what interpretation of a message is appropriate in a given context

TRUE/FALSE

Mark the statements below as true or false. For statements that are false, correct them on the lines below to create a true statement.

_____   1.   Words are not arbitrary symbols; they have meaning in and of themselves.

_____

_____   2.   Language can both *shape* our perceptions of the world and *reflect* our attitudes towards others.

_____

_____   3.   Since research shows that people are rated as more competent when their talk is free of powerless speech mannerisms, it is obvious that a consistently powerful style of speaking is always the best approach.

_____

_____   4.   Ambiguity and vagueness are forms of language that are to be avoided at all costs.

_____

_____   5.   If someone asks "Do you have the time?" and you do, it isn't appropriate to just say "yes." You must also say what time it is. This is an example of a semantic rule.

_____

_____   6.   "How are we feeling today?" is an example of "we" language.

_____

_____   7.   Naming children can be a way to express personal and ethnic identity.

_____

_____   8.   In a "but" statements, the word "but" seems to negate all that preceded it.

_____

_____ 9. Men are more likely to use language to accomplish a job, while women are more likely to use language to nourish relationships.

_____

_____ 10. A person from the United States is more likely to value direct language than is someone from Japan.

_____

COMPLETION

Fill in the blanks below with the correct terms chosen from the list below.

succinctness   equivocation   convergence   divergence   polite forms
tag questions   elaborateness   hedges   disclaimers   subscripting
formality   informality

1. _____is the process of adapting one's speech style to match that of others with whom the communicator wants to identify.

2. _____ in language use involve denying direct responsibility for the statement, such as "I could be wrong, but . . . "

3. _____ of language involve using respectful terms of address, such as "You're welcome, ma'am."

4. _____ involves speaking in a way that emphasizes a person's differences from the other persons with whom he or she is speaking .

5. _____ in language use involves using words that more than one commonly accepted definition, such as "They eat *healthy* food."

6. _____ in language use involve a negation statement, such as "*Didn't you think* that party was boring?"

7. _____ in language use make less of the feeling or intention statement, such as "I'm *rather* upset."

8. _____ in language use involves using a date or instance to reduce static evaluation, such as "Kanako is nervous."

9. _____ involves speaking with few words, and it is usually most extreme in cultures where silence is valued.

10. _____ involves speaking with rich and expressive terms, sometimes involving strong assertions and exaggerations.

11. _____ is a way of using correct grammar as a way of defining social position in some cultures.

12. _____ is a way of using language that is casually friendly and does not reflect a series of relational hierarchies in a particular culture.

MULTIPLE CHOICE

Label the examples of language given below by writing the letter of the language type illustrated on the line in front of the example.

a. inference   b. relative word   c. abstract words
d. emotive word   e. equivocal language

_____ 1. John didn't call **so he must be angry**.

_____ 2. I have a **stomach problem**.

_____ 3. That place is **expensive**.

_____ 4. That guy is a real **hunk**.

_____ 5. My car is **hot**. (Temperature inside? Overheating? Good-looking? Stolen?)

_____ 6. She left the meeting early; **she must have been irritated**.

_____ 7. When I said I'd always help **bail you out**, I didn't mean from jail, just that I'd help you pay your bills.

_____ 8. As your governor, I'd **improve education** in the state.

_____ 9. He showed up, **so he must agree with the protest**.

_____ 10. He's a real **tight-wad**.

_____ 11. All of the measures I've supported in Congress promote **security**.

_____ 12. Ian gave a **long** speech.

_____ 13. My grandfather is **young**.

_____ 14. My sister is a **pill**.

Choose the letter of the *least* abstract alternative to the high abstraction terms.

_____ 15. Jo's **constantly complaining**.
   a. Jo whines a lot.
   b. Jo complains often about the workload.
   c. Jo told me three times this week that she feels overworked.
   d. Every time we meet, Jo complains about all the work she does.

_____ 16. He can **never** do **anything** because he's **always busy**.
   a. He couldn't take me to dinner last night because he had to work.
   b. He can never do anything fun because he's always working.
   c. He didn't ever take time off to be with me.
   d. He works too much so we have a boring life.

_____ 17. There are **a lot of problems** associated with **freedom**.
   a. Freedom carries with it responsibility.

b. Since I moved into my own apartment, I have to pay ten bills.

c. I don't like all the responsibility of living on my own.

d. My economic responsibilities limit my freedom.

_____ 18. Shannon is **worthless** as a roommate.

a. Shannon is always gone, so she's really not part of our house.

b. Shannon never does her part around here.

c. Shannon's jobs seldom get done around here.

d. Shannon has attended only one of our six house meetings.

_____ 19. Carlos is the **most wonderful friend**.

a. Carlos has never told anyone about my fear of failing.

b. Carlos listens to me about everything.

c. Carlos is the best listener I've ever met.

d. I can trust Carlos implicitly with all my secrets.

_____ 20. Keiko **goes overboard** in trying to make people like her.

a. Keiko gave everyone on the team a valentine.

b. Keiko is the biggest kiss-up you ever met.

c. I think Keiko is trying to make my friends like her better than me.

d. I want Keiko to stop trying to outdo everybody else.

CHAPTER 5 STUDY GUIDE ANSWERS

CROSSWORD PUZZLE

```
              1r         2e  m  o  t  i  v  e         3l
         4d        e         q                        o
          e        l         u                        w
5a  6b  s  t  r  a  c  t  i  o  n               -        7d
  e     e        t         v                  c        i
  h     r        i         o                  o        v
  a     m        v       8c  o  n  v  e  r  g  e  n  c  e
  v     i        e         a               t        r
  i     n                  l       9s      e        g
  o     i                          y      x        e
10r  s  u 11b  s 12c  r 13i  p  t  i  n  g        t        n
  a     m        e        r        t              c
  l     e        l        a        a              e
        a        a        g        t
        n        t        m        i
        t        i        a        c
        i        v        t
        c        i        i
                 s        c
                 m
```

TRUE/FALSE

1. F	3. F	5. F	7. T	9. T
2. T	4. F	6. F	8. T	10. T

COMPLETION

1. convergence
2. disclaimers
3. polite forms
4. divergence
5. equivocation
6. tag questions
7. hedges
8. subscripting
9. succinctness
10. elaborateness
11. formality
12. informality

MULTIPLE CHOICE

1. a	5. e	9. a	13. b	17. b
2. c	6. a	10. d	14. d	18. d
3. b	7. e	11. c	15. c	19. a
4. d	8. c	12. b	16. a	20. a

C H A P T E R   S I X

Nonverbal Communication: Messages Beyond Words

OUTLINE

Use this outline to take notes as you read the chapter in the text and/or as your instructor lectures in class.

I. **CHARACTERISTICS OF NONVERBAL COMMUNICATION**
   A. **Nonverbal Skills are Important**
   B. **All Behavior Has Communicative Value**
      1. Deliberate
      2. Unintentional
   C. **Nonverbal Communication Is Primarily Relational**
      1. Managing identity
      2. Defining relationships
      3. Conveying emotion
   D. **Nonverbal Communication Serves Many Functions**
      1. Repeating
      2. Complementing
      3. Substituting
      4. Accenting
      5. Regulating
      6. Contradicting
      7. Deceiving - leakage
   E. **Nonverbal Communication Is Ambiguous**
      1. Silence
      2. Sexual behavior
      3. NVLD

II. **INFLUENCES ON NONVERBAL COMMUNICATION**
   A. **Gender**
      1. Physical and social
      2. Subordinate roles
      3. Cultural norms
   B. **Culture**
      1. Sending nonverbal messages
      2. interpreting nonverbal communication

III. **TYPES OF NONVERBAL COMMUNICATION**

A. Body Movement
   1. Body Orientation
      a. Facing toward or away
      b. Signals interest or exclusion
   2. Posture
      a. Emotions
      b. Tension/relaxation
   3. Gestures
      a. Illustrators
      b. Emblems
      c. Adaptors (manipulators)
   4. Face and Eyes
      a. Face: number, speed, microexpressions
      b. Eyes: Involvement, attitude, , dominance, interest

B. Voice (Paralanguage)
   1. Emphasis
   2. Tone, Speed, Pitch, Volume, Pauses, Disfluencies
   3. Sarcasm
   4. Credibility and liking

C. Touch (Haptics)
   1. Signals type of relationship
   2. Context matters: who, where, when
   3. Shapes responses: s liking
   4. Essential to development and health

D. Appearance
   1. Physical Attractiveness
   2. Clothing

E. Physical Space (proxcmics)
   1. Distance
      a. Intimate
      b. Personal
      c. Social
      d. Public
   2. Territoriality

F. Physical Environment
   1. Architecture and design
   2. Shaping interactions

G. Time (Chronemics)
   1. Status
   2. Culture: monochromic/polychronic

KEY TERMS

accenting

adaptors

body orientation

chronemics

complementing

contradicting

disfluencies

emblems

gestures

haptics

illustrators

intimate distance

kinesics

leakage

manipulators

microexpression

mixed message

monochromic

nonverbal communication

paralanguage

personal distance

polychromic

posture

proxemics

public distance

regulating

repeating

social distance

substituting

territory

ACTIVITIES

6.1 DESCRIBING NONVERBAL STATES
Activity Type: Skill Builder, Group Discussion

PURPOSE

To describe the nonverbal behaviors that indicate various emotional and attitudinal states.

INSTRUCTIONS

1. For each of the statements below, record the nonverbal behaviors that reflect the attitude or emotions described.
2. Compare your responses with those of others in the class and note the similarities and differences in your responses.
3. For each item, describe on as many types of nonverbal behavior as you can: Body Movement (orientation, posture, gestures, face/eyes), Voice, Touch, Appearance, Physical space, Physical environment, Time

.

EXAMPLE 1

He says I'm too eager to please.
I respond quickly after a request. I lean toward the person a lot. I smile and keep the smile on my face continuously. I gesture quickly. I stand a bit bowed over. I tilt my head to the side submissively.

EXAMPLE 2

She listens well.
Turns body toward me, leans forward, smiles once or twice, nods, maintains eye contact about 80 percent of the time.

1. My boss is mean.

_____

_____

2. My co-workers say I don't treat them well.

_____

_____

3. He's not into this project.

_____

_____

4. She can't stop flirting.

_____

_____

Designer: Wherever this exercise breaks and goes on to a second page, these words should appear at the top:

Body movement (orientation, posture, gestures, face/eyes), voice, touch, appearance, physical space, physical environment, time

5. They tell me I'm too tense.

_____

_____

6. She acts like she's in charge.

_____

_____

7. He makes a big deal of everything.

_____

_____

8. You need to act more sure of yourself.

_____

_____

9. He seems friendly.

_____

_____

10. You're not exactly a ray of sunshine.

_____

_____

11. They tell me I'm too aggressive.

_____

_____

12. She's "hyper."

_____

_____

List how at least two of the preceding statements could be taken in both positive and negative ways (*i.e., number 6 could be positive if you are grateful that she's organizing things, but negative if you're resentful of her influence*).

_____

_____

_____

_____

List the nonverbal behaviors that are associated with the alternate interpretation (the one you didn't record initially) and your reaction. (*i.e., I can see the positive side of taking charge – assigning seating, standing erect, firm voice, keeping to a time schedule, nodding and making eye contact with those who should speak to you. There's often a small difference between the nonverbal behaviors I find positive and those I find annoying or bossy*).

_____

_____

_____

_____

6.2 DESCRIBING NONVERBAL BEHAVIORS
Activity Type: Skill Builder, Group Discussion

PURPOSE

To explore effective nonverbal behavior and develop broader understanding of types of nonverbal behavior.

INSTRUCTIONS

1. For each of the social situations below, list the nonverbal behaviors you believe will achieve the stated goal.
2. Compare your answers with those of others in your class.
3. Reflect on the behavior of yourself and others important to you. How might you change some of the nonverbal cues you display to communicate what you desire more effectively?
4. Use as many categories of nonverbal behavior as you can: Body movement (orientation, posture, gestures, face/eyes), voice, touch, appearance, physical space, physical environment, time.

Example:

Initiate conversation with a stranger at a party.
Make eye contact, offer hand in greeting, smile, come within four feet of other person, turn body toward other person, nod occasionally when other is talking.

1. Take control or exercise leadership in a class group.

_____

_____

2. Come across well in a job interview.

_____

_____

3. Tell an interesting joke or story.

_____

_____

4. Appear friendly and warm without "coming on too strong."

_____

_____

5. Signal your desire to leave a conversation when the other person keeps on talking.

_____

_____

6. Appear confident when asking boss for a raise.

_____

_____

7. Appear interested in class lecture.

_____

_____

8. Avoid talking with a person on a plane or bus.

_____

_____

9. Show kindness toward an elderly relative.

_____

_____

10. Appear concerned about a friend's dilemma.

_____

_____

11. Describe two of your usual nonverbal behaviors in a particular context that you might want to change.

_____

_____

_____

_____

12. Why might you want to change them?

_____

_____

_____

_____

_____

6.3 AMBIGUITY, CONTRADICTION & CONGRUENCE

Activity Type: Invitation to Insight

PURPOSE

1. To analyze the verbal and nonverbal aspects of your communication behaviors.
2. To weigh the consequences of sending congruent, contradictory, or ambiguous messages.

INSTRUCTIONS

1. In each of the following situations, describe verbal and nonverbal behaviors likely to occur: body movement (orientation, posture, gestures, face/eyes), voice, touch, appearance, physical space, physical environment, time. Nonverbal behaviors seldom occur alone, so describe clusters of at least 3 nonverbal behaviors for each situation. Note whether the verbal and nonverbal behaviors are ambiguous (pages 205-207), contradictory (page 204) or congruent. Finally, evaluate the possible consequences of the ambiguity, contradictions or congruency.
2. Next describe situations from your own life and how you would send verbal and nonverbal messages. Include the possible consequences of your congruent or ambiguous behaviors.
3. After you've completed the examples, answer the questions about congruency/ambiguity.

SITUATION	YOUR VERBAL BEHAVIOR	YOUR NONVERBAL BEHAVIOR (USE A CLUSTER OF BEHAVIORS HERE)	ARE BEHAVIORS, CONTRADICTORY, AMBIGUOUS OR CONGRUENT?	POSSIBLE CONSEQUENCES
EXAMPLE Person I like a lot takes me out to dinner and I have a good time and enjoy the food.	"I'm really enjoying this; the food is terrific and so is the company."	I look at my partner when I talk, smiling and tilting my head, and leaning slightly forward. I touch my partner light on the arm and hand.	My verbal and nonverbal behaviors are congruent, not ambiguous.	I hope my partner will understand how much I care and enjoy our time together. I run the risk of being hurt if my partner's feelings don't match mine, but I'm willing to take that risk.
1. My boss asks me to work late when I've made other plans.				

Class_____   Name _____

SITUATION	YOUR VERBAL BEHAVIOR	YOUR NONVERBAL BEHAVIOR (USE A **CLUSTER** OF BEHAVIORS HERE)	ARE THE BEHAVIORS AMBIGUOUS?	POSSIBLE CONSEQUENCES
2. My roommate asks, while I'm doing homework, if I can make dinner.				
3. My relative drops in to visit me when other people are over for the evening.				
4. My romantic partner says I act like I'm indifferent when we discuss our future.				
5. Our waiter starts to take my plate and asks if I'm finished while food is still on my plate.				
6. (your example)				
7. (your example)				

8. (your example)				

Reflections.

1. Are there situations in which it is advantageous to express yourself ambiguously? Explain how sending one message verbally and another one nonverbally could be beneficial or explain why you believe it never is advantageous.

_____

_____

_____

_____

2. Describe situations in which ambiguity clearly is not desirable. Describe how you could best match your verbal and nonverbal behaviors in these situations.

_____

_____

_____

_____

3. What are the ethical considerations of nonverbal ambiguity or contradiction? Is it ever ethical to intentionally be ambiguous or contradictory? Why or why not? Can you think of situations in which it is never or ever ethical to intentionally send ambiguous or contradictory nonverbal messages?

_____

_____

_____

_____

4. Are there situations in which nonverbal ambiguity or contradiction is unintentional and unavoidable? Explain your answer

_____

_____

_____

_____

6.4 MEDIATED MESSAGES – NONVERBAL

Activity Type: Group Discussion

PURPOSE

To analyze nonverbal communication in mediated contexts.

INSTRUCTIONS

Discuss each of the questions below in your group. Prepare written answers for your instructor, or be prepared to contribute to a large group discussion, comparing your experiences with those of others in your class.

1. Mediated contexts often deprive us of important nonverbal communication cues. Discuss what nonverbal cues are present and absent in various mediated contexts (e.g., telephone, email, handwritten messages) used by members of your group.

   _____

   _____

2. List substitutions that people make for missing nonverbal cues in mediated contexts. How effective are these substitutions?

   _____

   _____

   _____

3. Your textbook discusses nonverbal signals of deception, or leakage. Describe why you think it is easier or more difficult to detect deception in mediated contexts.

   _____

   _____

4. Discuss the messages conveyed by the use of time in mediated contexts (for example, the length of time taken to return a phone call or an email). Include both intentional and unintentional messages.

   _____

   _____

5. What nonverbal cues convey the greatest meaning for you in phone calls? In text messages?

   _____

   _____

6.5 YOUR CALL—NONVERBAL
Activity Type: Group Discussion

PURPOSE

To analyze the possible interpretations of nonverbal behavior and how to respond to them.

INSTRUCTIONS

Use the case below and the discussion questions that follow to discuss the variety of communication issues involved in effective communication. Make notes on this page, add other pages on your own, or prepare a group report/analysis based on your discussion. Add your own experiences to individualize the analysis to make it **Your Call**.

CASE

Malena and Dolly are coworkers in different departments in a large company. Over coffee one day Malena tells Dolly that she's been feeling very uneasy lately about her boss's behavior. "I'm not exactly sure how to describe it," Malena says, "but I think he's 'coming on' to me, and I don't know what to do."

1. Malena would do well to be able to describe her boss's behavior. Imagine a situation like this and **describe** the possible behavior of Malena's boss.

_____

_____

2. Which of the behavior's listed in question 1 might be intentional and which might be unintentional? Why?

_____

_____

3. Describe possible intentional or unintentional nonverbal behaviors of Malena that might be misunderstood.

_____

_____

4. Using ideas from this and the previous chapters in the text, what could Malena do verbally and nonverbally to handle this issue?

_____

_____

_____

_____

STUDY GUIDE

CHECK YOUR UNDERSTANDING

CROSSWORD PUZZLE

ACROSS

1. a nonverbal function that emphasizes part of a verbal message
4. Hall's spatial zone from skin contact to 18 inches
7. a nonverbal function that manages whose turn it is to talk
8. nonverbal behavior cues that signal the untruthfulness of a verbal message
10. a deliberate nonverbal behavior with precise meaning known to virtually all members of a cultural group
15. the study of how humans use and structure time

16. the study of how people and animals use space

DOWN

2. nonverbal behavior that is inconsistent with a verbal message
3. a geographical area to which we assume some kind of "rights"
5. brief facial expressions
6. the study of body position and motion
7. an example of a personal territory within a house
9. nonverbal behavior that accompanies and supports verbal messages
11. movements of the hands and arms
12. the way in which individuals carry themselves: erect, slumping, etc.
13. nonverbal behaviors that reveal information a communicator does not disclose verbally
14. a nonlinguistic verbalization like um, er, ah

TRUE/FALSE

Mark the statements below as true or false. Correct statements that are false on the lines below to create a true statement.

_____   1. Nonverbal behaviors are, by their nature, intentional.

_____

_____   2. Nonverbal communication encompasses abstract factors such as physical appearance, the environment in which we communicate, and the way we use time.

_____

_____   3. The concept of nonverbal convergence illustrates that skilled communicators can adapt their behavior when interacting with members of other cultures or co-cultures in order to make the exchange more effective.

_____

_____   4. Nonverbal communication is much better suited to expressing attitudes and feelings than it is to expressing concrete ideas.

_____

_____   5. Research on nonverbal communication and lying shows that individuals who are trying to deceive others are less likely to show nonverbal evidence of lying if they haven't had a chance to rehearse their lying and when they feel strongly about the information being hidden.

_____

_____   6. In studies of detecting lying, men are consistently more accurate than women at detecting the lies and discovering the underlying truth.

_____

_____   7.   Both verbal and nonverbal messages are communicated one at a time, rather like pearls on a string.

_____

_____   8.   Unlike verbal communication that is intermittent (starts and stops), nonverbal communication is continuous and never ending.

_____

_____   9.   The nonverbal impact of messages is more powerful than the verbal impact.

_____

_____   10. Nonverbal communication is clearer than verbal communication.

_____

_____   11. The concept of leakage is most often associated with deception.

_____

_____   12. The main reason we miss most posture messages is that they are so obvious.

_____

_____   13. Behaviors that have one meaning for members of the same culture or co-culture can be interpreted differently by members of another group.

_____

_____   14. Women are more likely to believe the deception of an intimate partner than are men.

_____

_____   15. When you use nonverbal behavior to regulate other's behavior, it guarantees that the other will pay attention to, interpret, or respond as you intended.

_____

_____

COMPLETION

Fill in the blanks below with the correct terms chosen from the list below.

illustrator	intimate	personal	social	public
relaxation	paralanguage	emblem	adaptor	touch
body orientation	nonverbal learning disorder			

1.   _____ is the distance zone identified by Hall that ranges from four to about twelve feet; within it are the kinds of communication that usually occur in business.

2.   _____ is a postural cue such as leaning back or lowering shoulders that a higher status person usually exhibits when not feeling threatened.

3. _____ is a deliberate, nonverbal behavior that has a very precise meaning known to virtually everyone within a cultural group.

4. _____ is the distance zone identified by Hall that ranges from eighteen inches to four feet and includes behavior found in most social conversations.

5. _____ is a gesture that accompanies speech but doesn't stand on its own.

6. _____ is the degree to which we face toward or away from someone with our body, feet, and head.

7. _____ is the distance zone identified by Hall that ranges from skin contact to about eighteen inches; we usually use this distance with people in private who are emotionally very close to us.

8. _____ is the distance zone identified by Hall that ranges from twelve feet outward and includes communication such as that found in a typical classroom.

9. _____ is nonverbal behavior that includes having a foreign accent.

10. _____ is nonverbal behavior that includes brushing up against someone.

11. _____ is an unconscious body movement that helps us adjust to the environment.

12. _____ is a syndrome that makes reading nonverbal cues more difficult.

MULTIPLE CHOICE

Choose the letter of the type of nonverbal communication that is illustrated below.

a. environment   b. paralinguistics   c. proxemics   d. territoriality

_____ 1. No one dared to sit in Ralph's chair.
_____ 2. Jeremy put a "NO ENTRANCE" sign on his door.
_____ 3. The students rearranged the chairs in the classroom.
_____ 4. Manuela stepped back three feet from her friend.
_____ 5. The lovers were sitting only inches apart.
_____ 6. Rob's voice softened when he spoke to her.
_____ 7. There was a long pause after the decision was made.
_____ 8. Mitchell sighed audibly.
_____ 9. Gretchen took the third seat down from Yayoi.
_____ 10. Kevin was annoyed that someone was leaning on his car.

a. body orientation   b. gesture   c. touch   d. face and eyes

_____ 11. The children playfully kicked one another.

_____ 12. Professor Jimenez illustrated her lecture with many arm movements.

_____ 13. Leland shifted his shoulders toward the speaker.

_____ 14. Ernie avoided looking at her.

_____ 15. The executive stared at her employee.

_____ 16. Martin turned his body away from his brother.

_____ 17. The officer pointed in the correct direction.

_____ 18. Letoya didn't appreciate the slap on the back.

_____ 19. Blake set his jaw in disgust.

_____ 20. Francesca signaled "OK" across the room.

CHAPTER 6 STUDY GUIDE ANSWERS

CROSSWORD PUZZLE

Across/Down answers shown in grid:

- 1 accenting
- 4 intimate
- 7 regulate
- 8 deceiving
- 10 emblem
- 15 chronemics
- 16 proxemics

Down entries: contradicting, territory, mirror, kinesics, gestures, posture, leakage, disclosure, etc.

TRUE/FALSE

1. F	4. T	7. F	10. F	13. T
2. T	5. F	8. T	11. T	14. T
3. T	6. F	9. T	12. F	15. F

COMPLETION

1. social	5. illustrator	9. paralanguage
2. relaxation	6. body orientation	10. touch
3. emblem	7. intimate	11. adaptor

4. personal   8. public   12. nonverbal learning disorder

MULTIPLE CHOICE

1. d	5. c	9. c	13. a	17. b
2. d	6. b	10. d	14. d	18. c
3. a	7. b	11. c	15. d	19. d
4. c	8. b	12. b	16. a	20. b

C H A P T E R   S E V E N

Listening: More Than Meets the Ear

OUTLINE

Use this outline to take notes as you read the chapter in the text or as your instructor lectures in class.

I. LISTENING DEFINED
  A. Hearing vs. listening
  B. Mindless listening
  C. Mindful listening

II. ELEMENTS IN THE LISTENING PROCESS
  A. **Hearing - Physiological**
  B. **Attending - Psychological**
  C. **Understanding – Making Sense**
  D. **Responding – Observable Feedback**
  E. **Remembering - Recalling**

III. THE CHALLENGE OF LISTENING
  A. **Types of ineffective listening**
    1. Pseudolistening
    2. Stage Hogging
    3. Selective Listening
    4. Insulated Listening
    5. Defensive Listening
    6. Ambushing
    7. Insensitive Listening
  B. Why we don't listen better
    1. Message Overload
    2. Preoccupation
    3. Rapid Thought
    4. Effort
    5. External Noise
    6. Faulty Assumptions
    7. Lack of Apparent Advantages
    8. Lack of Training
    9. Hearing problems
    10. Media Influences
  C. Meeting the challenge of listening better

1. Talk Less
2. Get Rid of Distractions
3. Don't Judge Prematurely
4. Look for Key Ideas

IV. TYPES OF LISTENING RESPONSES

A. Prompting: encouraging

B. Questioning: clarifying

1. Ask sincere questions
2. Avoid counterfeit questions that
   a. trap the speaker
   b. tag questions
   c. make statements
   d. carry hidden agendas
   e. seek "correct" answers
   f. are based on unchecked assumptions

C. Paraphrasing: reflecting understanding

1. Factual information
2. Personal information
   a.. Change the speaker's wording
   b. Offer an example
   c. Reflect the underlying theme
3. Remain tentative
4. Use sparingly
   a. If the problem is complex enough
   b. If you have necessary time and concern
   c. If you can withhold judgment
   d. If it is proportional

D. Supporting: expressing solidarity

1. Types
   a. Empathizing
   b. Agreement
   c. Offers to help
   d. Praise
   e. Reassurance
2. Potential problems ("cold comfort")
   a. Denying others the right to their feelings
   b. minimizing the significance of the situation
   c. focusing on "then and there" not "here and now"
   d. casting judgment
   e. defending yourself
3. Guidelines
   a. Approval not necessary
   b. Monitor reaction
   c. Support not always welcome

E. Analyzing: interpreting

1. Be tentative
2. Have chance of being correct
3. Receptive other
4. Motivated to be helpful

F. Advising: offering a solution

1. Be accurate
2. Be sure other is ready to accept
3. Best if blame is not likely
4. Deliver supportively, in a face-saving manner

G. Judging: evaluating

1. Be sure judgment is asked for
2. Be genuinely constructive

H. Choosing the best listening response

1. Gender
2. The situation
3. The other person
4. Your personal style

KEY TERMS

advising response
ambushing
analyzing response
attending
counterfeit questions
defensive listening
hearing
insensitive listening
insulated listening
judging response
listening
mindful listening
mindless listening
paraphrasing

prompting
pseudolistening
questioning response
remembering
responding
selective listening
sincere questions
stage-hogging
supportive response
understanding

ACTIVITIES

7.1 LISTENING DIARY

Activity Type: Invitation to Insight

PURPOSES

1. To identify the styles of listening you use in your interpersonal relationships.
2. To discover the consequences of the listening styles you use.

BACKGROUND

Looking Out/Looking In identifies several styles of effective and ineffective listening that you can use when listening to others:

pseudolistening	insensitive listening	supporting
stage hogging	ambushing	analyzing
selective listening	prompting	advising
insulated listening	questioning	judging
defensive listening	paraphrasing	

INSTRUCTIONS

1. Use the following form to record the listening styles you use in various situations.
2. After completing your diary, record your conclusions.

TIME AND PLACE	PEOPLE	SUBJECT	LISTENING STYLE(S)	CONSEQUENCES
EXAMPLE *Saturday night party*	*My date and several new acquaintances*	*Good backpacking trips*	*Stage-hogging: I steered everybody's remarks around to my own experiences*	*I guess I was trying to get everyone to like me, but my egotistical attitude probably accomplished the opposite.*
1.				
2.				

144

	TIME AND PLACE	PEOPLE	SUBJECT	LISTENING STYLE(S)	CONSEQUENCES
3.					
4.					

Based on your observations, what styles of effective and ineffective listening do you use most often? In what situations do you use each of these styles? (Consider the people involved, the time, subject, and your personal mood when determining situational variables.)

_____

_____

_____

_____

What are the consequences of using the listening styles you have just described?

_____

_____

_____

What other listening styles might increase your effectiveness? Why?

_____

_____

_____

7.2 EFFECTIVE QUESTIONING

Activity Type: Skill Builder

PURPOSE

To develop your ability to question effectively in order to gain information about another person's thoughts.

INSTRUCTIONS

1. For each of the following statements, write two questions to get more information. Avoid counterfeit questions that trap the speaker, carry hidden agendas, seek "correct" answers, or are based on unchecked assumptions.
2. Enter statement examples of your own and two questions each to solicit information.

EXAMPLE

"It's not fair that I have to work so much. Other students can get better grades because they have the time to study."
How do you feel when others score higher than you?
How many hours a week do you work?

1. "I guess it's OK for you to use my computer, but you have to understand that I've put a lot of time and money into it."

    _____

    _____

2. "You'll have the best chance at getting a loan for the new car you want if you give us a complete financial statement and credit history."

    _____

    _____

3. (Instructor to student) "This paper shows a lot of promise. It could probably earn you an A grade if you just develop the idea about the problems that arise from poor listening a bit more."

    _____

    _____

4. "I do like the communication course, but it's not at all what I expected. It's much more *personal*, if you know what I mean."

    _____

    _____

5. "We just got started on your car's transmission. I'm pretty sure we can have it ready tonight."

_____

_____

6. "I do think it's wrong to take any lives, but sometimes I think certain criminals deserve capital punishment."

_____

_____

7. "My son never tells me what's going on in his life. And now he's moving away."

_____

_____

8. "My family is so controlling. They make it impossible for me to escape."

_____

_____

9. "It was a great game, I guess.   I played a lot, but only scored once. The coach put Ryan in ahead of me."

_____

_____

10. "We had a great evening last night. The dinner was fantastic; so was the party. We saw lots of people. Erin loves that sort of thing."

_____

_____

11. (Your example)_____

_____

_____

12. (Your example)_____

_____

_____

7.3 PARAPHRASING

Activity Type: Skill Builder

PURPOSE

To create paraphrasing responses to others' problems.

BACKGROUND

The most helpful paraphrasing responses reflect both the speaker's thoughts and feelings. In order for this style of helping to be effective, you also have to sound like yourself, and not another person or a robot. There are many ways to reflect another's thoughts and feelings:

"It sounds like you're . . ."   "And so . . . "
"I hear you saying . . ."   "Is it that . . . "
"Let me see if I've got it. You're saying . . ."   "Are you . . ."
"So you're telling me . . ."   "Could you mean . . ."

Leave your paraphrase open (tentative) by using words that invite the speaker to clarify or correct your paraphrase (ex: "Is that right?")

INSTRUCTIONS

Write a paraphrasing response for each of the statements that follow. Be sure that the response fits your style of speaking, while at the same time it reflects the speaker's *thoughts* and *feelings*.

EXAMPLE

"Stan always wants to tell me about the woman he's currently going out with or the project he's currently working on. He gives me details that take hours, but he rarely asks about who I'm going out with or what I'm interested in."

"It seems like you might be tired (feeling) of hearing about Stan's love life (thoughts) and maybe a little put-out (feeling) that he doesn't solicit information from you about whom you're dating (thoughts) — is that it?"

1. "I hate this instructor. First she told me my paper was too short, so I gave her more information. Now she tells me it's too wordy."

    _____

    _____

    _____

2. "I worked up that whole study — did all the surveying, the compiling, the writing. It was my idea in the first place. But he turned it in to the head office with his name on it, and he got the credit."

    _____

    _____

    _____

3. "We can't decide whether to put Grandmother in a nursing home. She hates the idea, but she can't take care of herself anymore, and it's just too much for us."

_____

_____

_____

4. "She believed everything he said about me. She wouldn't even listen to my side—just started yelling at me. I thought we were better friends than that."

_____

_____

_____

5. "I'm really starting to hate my job. Every day I do the same boring, mindless work. But if I quit, I might not find any better work."

_____

_____

_____

6. "My girlfriend hasn't called me in forever. I think she must be mad at me."

_____

_____

_____

7. "How can I tell him how I really feel? He might get mad, and then we'd start arguing. He'll think I don't love him if I tell him my real feelings. I'm at a loss."

_____

_____

_____

8. "Why don't you try to be a little less messy around here? This place looks like a dump to all our friends."

_____

_____

_____

9. "There's no reasoning with him. All he cares about is his image—not all the work I have to do to cover for him."

_____

_____

_____

10. "You'd think someone who loves you would take off to be with you now and then, wouldn't you?"

_____

_____

_____

11. "This new software program is supposed to save time? That's a joke."

_____

_____

_____

12. "He acts as if staying home with two children all day is easy. I'm more tired now than when I worked full-time – and I got paid then and had weekends and evenings off!"

_____

_____

_____

13. "My father is so needy since my mother died. I have no life of my own any more."

_____

_____

_____

14. "Group projects are a nightmare. There should be a warning sign for classes that require them."

_____

_____

_____

7.4 LISTENING CHOICES

Activity Type: Skill Builder

PURPOSE

To practice different listening styles in responding to others.

INSTRUCTIONS

For each of the problem statements below, write a response in each style of helping discussed in *Looking Out/Looking In*. Make your response as realistic as possible. Then record a situation of your own and write listening responses for it.

EXAMPLE

"I don't know what to do. I tried to explain to my professor why the assignment was late, but he wouldn't even listen to me."
Prompting *(Short silence) And so . . . ? (Look expectantly at partner).*
Questioning *What did he say? Can you make up the assignment? How do you feel about this?*
Paraphrasing *You sound really discouraged, since he didn't even seem to care about your reasons – is that it?*
Supporting *All of your work has been so good that I'm sure this one assignment won't matter. Don't worry!*
Analyzing *I think the reason he wasn't sympathetic is because he hears lots of excuses this time of year.*
Advising *You ought to write him a note. He might be more open if he has time to read it and think about it.*
Judging *You have to accept these things. Moping won't do any good, so quit feeling sorry for yourself.*

---

1. My girlfriend says she wants to date other guys this summer while I'm away, working construction. She claims it's just to keep busy and that it won't make any difference with us, but I think she wants to break off permanently, and she's trying to do it gently.

    Prompting _____

    Questioning _____

    _____

    Paraphrasing _____

    _____

    Supporting _____

    _____

    Analyzing _____

    _____

    Advising _____

    _____

Judging _____

_____

Which listening styles do you think are most appropriate in this situation? Why?

_____

_____

_____ -

Which listening styles do you think are most inappropriate in this situation? Why?

_____

_____

_____

2. My roommate and I can't seem to get along. She's always having her boyfriend over, and he doesn't know when to go home. I don't want to move out, but I can't put up with this much longer. If I bring it up I know my roommate will get defensive, though.

Prompting _____

Questioning _____

_____

Paraphrasing _____

_____

Supporting _____

_____

Analyzing _____

_____

Advising _____

_____

Judging _____

_____

Which listening styles do you think are most appropriate in this situation? Why?

_____

_____

_____ -

Which listening styles do you think are most inappropriate in this situation? Why?

_____

_____

_____

3.   The pressure of going to school and doing all the other things in my life is really getting to me. I can't go on like this, but I don't know where I can cut back. What would be your long and short term goals in this situation? _____

_____

Circle the type of response you think will help you meet your goals: {Prompting, questioning, paraphrasing, supporting, analyzing, advising, judging} Why do you think this is the best type of listening response? _____

_____

Now write this type of response. _____

_____

4.   You think that by the time you become an adult your parents would stop treating you like a child, but not mine! If I wanted their advice about how to live my life, I'd ask.
What would be your long and short term goals in this situation?

_____

_____

Circle the type of response you think will help you meet your goals: {Prompting, questioning, paraphrasing, supporting, analyzing, advising, judging} Why do you think this is the best type of listening response? _____

_____

Now write this type of response. _____

_____

5. (record a situation of your own here) _____

_____

What would be your long and short term goals in this situation?

_____

_____

Circle the type of response you think will help you meet your goals: {Prompting, questioning, paraphrasing, supporting, analyzing, advising, judging} Why do you think this is the best type

of listening response? _____

_____

Now write this type of response. _____

_____

Reflections.

1. Are there types of listening responses that you are familiar with that are not mentioned here?

_____

_____

_____

2. Are there listening responses that you have trouble categorizing? Which ones? Why are they

difficult to categorize?

_____

_____

_____

3. Is there value to learning these categories? Why or why not?

_____

_____

_____

7.5 INFORMATIONAL LISTENING

Activity Type: Skill Builder

INSTRUCTIONS

1. Join with three partners to create a foursome. Label the members A, B, C, and D.
2. A and B review the list below, choosing the topic upon which they disagree most widely.
3. A and B conduct a five-minute conversation on the topic they have chosen. During this period, the speakers may not express their own ideas until they have effectively questioned and then paraphrased the other person's position to his or her satisfaction. (If A and B finish discussing one item, they should move on to a second one from the list below.)
   C observes A   D observes B
4. At the end of the conversation, the observers should review the listening with the persons they observed.
5. Repeat steps 1–5 with the roles of conversationalists and observers reversed.

TOPICS

Indicate your position on each statement below by circling one of the following labels:

TA = totally agree   A = agree   D = disagree   TD = totally disagree

1. Despite the value of classes like this one, in the last analysis, good communicators are born, not made.	TA	A	D	TD
2. One measure of a person's effectiveness as a communicator is how well he or she is liked by others.	TA	A	D	TD
3. No matter how unreasonable or rude they are, people deserve to be treated with respect.	TA	A	D	TD
4. An effective communicator should be able to handle any any situation in a way that leaves the other person feeling positive about the interaction.	TA	A	D	TD
5. Interpersonal communication classes should be a required part of everyone's college education.	TA	A	D	TD
6. Most of what is taught in interpersonal communication classes is really just common sense.	TA	A	D	TD

OR as an alternative

1. Choose a topic of interest to you and a partner (music, politics, religion, men, women, morals, etc.). It is best if you anticipate some difference of opinion on the topic.
2. Take turns stating your opinion. The only rule is that before you can take your turn stating *your* opinion, you must effectively question and paraphrase the content of your partner's opinion *to his or her satisfaction.*

7.6 LISTENING AND RESPONDING STYLES

Activity Type: Oral Skill

PURPOSE

To give you practice in using different listening styles to enhance listening effectiveness.

INSTRUCTIONS

1. With a partner, decide on communication situations that require effective listening. The situations should be real for the person describing them and might involve a problem, a decision that needs to be made, an issue of importance, or a change in a relationship.
2. Have your partner tell you the problem/issue/decision/relationship while you listen effectively.
3. You then tell your partner of your problem/issue/decision/relationship while your partner listens effectively.
4. Analyze the listening styles you used. Which were most/least effective in this situation? Which styles do you need to work on?
5. Use the checklist below to evaluate listening effectiveness.

CHECKLIST

Uses appropriate language and nonverbal behaviors that   _____
    -demonstrate genuine interest
    -seem compatible with your personal communication style
    -don't create defensiveness

Chooses the best balance of the responses, as appropriate   _____
    prompting
    genuine questioning
    paraphrasing
    concisely and clearly reflects speaker's *thoughts*
    concisely and clearly reflects speaker's *feelings*
    requests confirmation of paraphrase accuracy
    supporting (comforting, praising, agreeing, humor)
    analyzing
    advising
    judging

Based on self-observation (class feedback, videotape, etc.) and personal reflection   _____
   1. Which listening styles did you rely on most in this situation? Why?
   2. Which listening styles were most effective in this situation? Why?
   3. Which listening styles were least effective in this situation? Why?
   4. Predict how the conversation would have been different if you had used one or two other listening styles.

                                         Total   _____

7.7 MEDIATED MESSAGES--LISTENING

Activity Type: Group Discussion

PURPOSE

To analyze listening behaviors in mediated contexts.

INSTRUCTIONS

Discuss each of the questions below in your group. Prepare written answers for your instructor, or be prepared to contribute to a large group discussion, comparing your experiences with those of others in your class.

1. Media influence our listening or nonlistening. Record difficulties (focusing, attention span) that your group members have experienced with listening to various media.

_____

_____

_____

2. Describe ineffective listening styles (pseudolistening, selective, defensive, etc.) that your group thinks are more predominant in particular mediated contexts.

_____

_____

_____

3. Is listening ever more effective through mediated channels. Explain.

_____

_____

_____

4. What are the most important steps you believe people could take to make their listening in mediated channels more effective?

_____

_____

_____

7.8 YOUR CALL--LISTENING
Activity Type: Group Discussion

PURPOSE

To evaluate the appropriateness of different listening styles in a relationship.

INSTRUCTIONS

Use the case below and the discussion questions that follow to discuss the variety of communication issues involved in effective communication. Make notes on this page, add other pages on your own, or prepare a group report/analysis based on your discussion. Add your own experiences to individualize the analysis to make it **Your Call.**

CASE

Larry and Sam have been friends since elementary school and are now in their thirties. Larry has been happily married for ten years. Sam has been engaged four times, and each time has broken it off as the marriage date approaches. Sam has just announced another engagement.

1. What are the likely barriers that would prevent Larry from listening effectively?

_____

_____

2. What types of ineffective listening are likely to occur if Larry doesn't carefully consider his listening options?

_____

_____

_____

3. What listening style(s) could Larry use that would be most helpful to Sam? Why?   Construct a response for Larry using that style.

_____

_____

_____

4. Suppose that the two friends described here are both women. How would your responses to the preceding questions change?

_____

_____

_____

STUDY GUIDE

CHECK YOUR UNDERSTANDING

CROSSWORD PUZZLE

ACROSS

4. an imitation of true listening in which the receiver's mind is elsewhere
6. a response style in which the receiver perceives a speaker's comments as an attack
7. restating a speaker's thoughts and feelings in the listener's own words
8. a helping response in which the receiver offers suggestions about how the speaker should deal with a problem
10. using silences and brief statements of encouragement to draw out a speaker

12. the physiological dimension of listening
14. a response style in which the receiver responds only to messages that interest him or her
15. an ineffective listening style in which the listener accepts the speaker's words at face value, resulting in failure to recognize the thoughts or feelings that are not directly expressed by the speaker
16. a listening response that offers an interpretation of a speaker's message
17. a reaction in which the receiver evaluates the sender's message either favorably or unfavorably

DOWN
1. a style of listening in which the receiver seeks additional information from the sender
2. giving observable feedback to the speaker
3. occurs when sense is made of a message
5. a response style in which the receiver reassures, comforts, or distracts the person seeking help
9. a response in which the words of the speaker are repeated
11. a type of question that honestly seeks information without leading the speaker
13. an ineffective listening style in which the receiver ignores undesirable information

TRUE/FALSE

Mark the statements below as true or false. On the lines below each statement, correct the false statements by making a true statement.

_____ 1. We spend more time listening to others than in any other type of communication.

_____ 2. Speaking is active; listening is passive.

_____ 3. All interruptions are attempts at stage-hogging.

_____ 4. Mindful listening requires careful and thoughtful attention and responses.

_____ 5. In careful listening, the heart rate quickens and respiration increases.

_____ 6. People speak at about the same rate as others are capable of understanding their speech.

_____ 7. The advantages of listening are more obvious to people than the advantages of speaking.

_____ 8. Responding to a message rarely involves giving observable feedback to the speaker.

_____ 9. Judging as a listening response may be favorable or negative.

_____ 10. Even an accurate form of analytic listening can create defensiveness since it may imply superiority and evaluativeness.

COMPLETION

Fill in the blanks below with the correct terms chosen from the list below.

residual message	attending	conversational narcissist
sincere question	counterfeit question	constructive criticism
agreement	understanding	remembering
hearing	selective	insulated

1. _____ is a name given to a nonlistening stage-hog.

2. _____ is a genuine request for new information aimed at understanding others.

3. _____ is the information we store (remember) after processing information from teachers, friends, radio, TV, and other sources.

4. _____ is the psychological process of listening.

5. _____ is a query that is a disguised attempt to send a message, not receive one.

6. _____ is a lesser form of negative judgment which is intended to help the problem-holder improve in the future.

7. _____ is the physiological process of listening.

8. _____ is the process of making sense of a message.

9. _____ is the ability to recall information.

10. _____ is a listening response designed to show solidarity with speakers by telling them how right they are.

11. _____ is a nonlistening style that responds only to what the listener cares about.

12. _____ is a nonlistening style that ignores information the listener doesn't to deal with.

MULTIPLE CHOICE

Match the letter of the listening type with its example found below.

a. advising   c. analyzing   e. supporting   g. paraphrasing
b. judging   d. questioning   f. prompting

_____ 1. "So what do you mean by that?"

_____ 2. "You're mad at me for postponing the meeting?"

_____ 3. "You're probably just more upset than usual because of the stress of exams."

_____ 4. "What reason did she give for not attending?"

_____ 5. "Well, that was good of him not to complain."

_____ 6. "Have you tried praising her?"

_____ 7. "Have you tried talking to him about it?"

_____ 8. "Are you as excited as you sound about this big meet?"

_____ 9. "Jim should not have said that to Amy after you asked him not to."

_____ 10. "And then what happened?"

_____ 11. "So why did you go to Ellie's in the first place?"

_____ 12. "You really are good; they'll recognize that."

_____ 13. "It's not fair for you to have to work nights."

_____ 14. "Maybe you should give her a taste of her own medicine."

_____ 15. "And so you feel like retaliating because you're hurt?"

_____ 16. "Maybe you're a little insecure because of the divorce?"

_____ 17. "Like what?"

_____ 18. "What makes you think that he's cheating?"

_____ 19. "You've always pulled out those grades before—I know you can do it again."

_____ 20. "She's probably jealous so that's why she's doing that."

Choose the best listening response to each statement below.

21. Boss to employee: "Draft a letter that denies this request for a refund, but make it tactful."
Identify the best paraphrasing of content response.

    a. "What do you want me to say?"
    b. "How can I say no tactfully?"
    c. "So I should explain nicely why we can't give a refund, right?"
    d. "In other words, you want me to give this customer the brush-off?"

22. Friend says, "How do they expect us to satisfy the course requirements when there aren't enough spaces in the classes we're supposed to take?" Identify the best questioning response.

    a. "What class do you need that you can't get into?"
    b. "You think that some of the courses are worthless—is that it?"
    c. "Sounds like you're sorry you chose this major."
    d. "Why don't you write a letter to the chairperson of the department?"

23. Friend says, "Why don't I meet you after class at the student union?" Identify the best questioning response.

    a. "So you want me to pick you up at the student union?"
    b. "You want me to pick you up *again*?"
    c. "What time do you think you'll be there?"
    d. "Why can't you drive yourself? Is your car broken again?"

24. Co-worker advises, "When you go in for a job interview, be sure and talk about the internship, your coursework, and your extracurricular activities. Don't expect them to ask you." Identify the best paraphrasing response.

    a. "You think they won't ask about those things?"
    b. "Won't that sound like bragging?"
    c. "Why should I talk about the internship?"
    d. "So you're saying not to be bashful about stressing my experience?"

25. Friend says, "I don't think it's right that they go out and recruit women when there are plenty of good men around." Identify the best supporting response.

    a. "I think you're job-hunting well in spite of the challenges."
    b. "You shouldn't let that bother you."
    c. "That's just the way life is."
    d. "I can see that you're angry. What makes you think women are being given an unfair advantage?"

For each of the statements below, identify which response is the most complete and accurate paraphrasing of the speaker's thoughts and feelings.

26. "Sometimes I think I'd like to drop out of school, but then I start to feel like a quitter."

    a. "Maybe it would be helpful to take a break. You can always come back, you know."
    b. "You're afraid that you might fail if you stay in school now, is that it?"
    c. "I can really relate to what you're saying. I feel awkward here myself sometimes."
    d. "So you'd feel ashamed of yourself if you quit now, even though you'd like to?"

27. "I don't want to go to the party. I won't know anyone there, and I'll wind up sitting by myself all night."

    a. "You're anxious about introducing yourself to people who don't know you?"
    b. "You never know; you could have a great time."
    c. "So you really don't want to go, eh?"
    d. "What makes you think it will be that way?"

28. "I get really nervous talking to my professor. I keep thinking that I sound stupid."

    a. "Talking to her is really a frightening experience?"
    b. "You're saying that you'd rather not approach her?"

     c.   "You get the idea that she's evaluating you, so you feel inadequate?

     d.   "You think that talking to her might affect your grade for the worse?"

29.   "I don't know what to do about my kids. Their whining is driving me crazy."

     a.   "Even though whining is natural, it's getting to you?"

     b.   "Sometimes you lose patience and feel irritated when they complain?"

     c.   "You're getting angry at them?"

     d.   "Even the best parents get irritated sometimes."

30.   "I just blew another test in that class. Why can't I do better?"

     a.   "You probably need to study harder. You'll get it!"

     b.   "You're feeling sorry for yourself because you can't pull a better grade?"

     c.   "Where do you think the problem is?"

     d.   "You're discouraged and frustrated because you don't know what you're doing wrong?"

CHAPTER 7 STUDY GUIDE ANSWERS

CROSSWORD PUZZLE

Across:
- 4. pseudolistening
- 6. defensive
- 7. paraphrasing
- 8. advising
- 10. prompting
- 12. hearing
- 14. selecting
- 15. insensitive
- 16. analyzing
- 17. judging

Down:
- 1. questioning
- 2. responding
- 3. understanding
- 5. supporting
- 9. devise
- 11. sincere
- 13. instimulate

TRUE/FALSE

1. T	3. F	5. T	7. F	9. T
2. F	4. T	6. F	8. F	10. T

COMPLETION

1. conversational narcissist
2. sincere question
5. counterfeit question
6. constructive criticism
9. remembering
10. agreement

3. residual message
4. attending

7. hearing
8. understanding

11. selective
12. insulated

MULTIPLE CHOICE

1. f	7. a	13. b	19. e	25. a
2. g	8. g	14. a	20. c	26. d
3. c	9. b	15. g	21. c	27. a
4. d	10. f	16. c	22. a	28. c
5. b	11. d	17. f	23. c	29. b
6. a	12. e	18. d	24. d	30. d

C H A P T E R   E I G H T

Communication and Relational Dynamics

OUTLINE

Use this outline to take notes as you read the chapter in the text or as your instructor lectures in class.

I. WHY WE FORM RELATIONSHIPS

    A. Appearance

    B. Similarity

    C. Complementarity

    D. Reciprocal attraction

    E. Competence

    F. Disclosure

    G. Proximity

    H. Rewards: Social exchange theory

II. RELATIONAL DEVELOPMENT AND MAINTENANCE

    A. Models of Relational Development

        1. Developmental Models illustrate coming together, coming apart and/or relational maintenance (Knapp)

            a. Initiating

            b. Experimenting

            c. Intensifying

            d. Integrating

            e. Bonding

            f. Differentiating

            g. Circumscribing

            h. Stagnating

            i. Avoiding

            j. Terminating

        2. Dialectical Perspectives/tensions

            a. Connection vs. autonomy

            b. Openness vs. privacy

            c. Predictability vs. novelty

            d. Managing dialectical tensions

                a) Denial

                b) Disorientation

                c) Alternation

                d) Segmentation

     e) Balance
     f) Integration
     g) Recalibration
     h) Reaffirmation

  B. Characteristics of Relationships
    1. Relationships are constantly changing
    2. Relationships are affected by culture
    3. Relationships require maintenance
     a. positivity
     b. openness
     c. assurances
     d. social networks
     e. sharing tasks

  C. Repairing Damaged Relationships
    1. Types of relational transgressions
     a. minor vs. significant
     b. social vs. relational
     c. deliberate vs. unintentional
     d. one-time vs. incremental

    2. Strategies for relational repair
     a. acknowledgement
     b. apology
     c. compensation

    3. Forgiving transgressions

III. COMMUNICATING ABOUT RELATIONSHIPS

  A. Content and Relational Messages
    1. Content: subject
    2. Relational: feelings
  B. Types of Relational Messages
    1. Affinity
    2. Immediacy
    3. Respect
    4. Control
     a. Decisional
     b. Conversational
  C. Metacommunication

KEY TERMS

affinity
avoiding
bonding
circumscribing
connection-autonomy dialectic
content message
control
dialectical tension
differentiating
experimenting
immediacy
initiating

integrating
intensifying
metacommunication
openness-privacy dialectic
predictability-novelty dialectic
relational maintenance
relational message
relational transgressions
respect
stagnating
terminating

ACTIVITIES

8.1 DISCOVERING DIALECTICS
Activity Type: Invitation to Insight

PURPOSE

To identify and describe behaviors that contribute to dialectical tensions in relationships.

INSTRUCTIONS

1. Identify the dialectical tensions operating in the situations below, taking time to explain the conflicting feelings and thoughts in each: *Connection vs. autonomy, Openness vs. privacy, Predictability vs. novelty* .
2. Identify one or more of the eight strategies for managing dialectical tensions (*denial, disorientation, alternation, segmentation, balance,, integration, recalibration, and reaffirmation*) that you believe would be most beneficial to the relationship, and explain how the relationship would deal with the dialectical tension under these circumstances.
3. Describe dialectical tensions at work in your own relationships and label and explain the strategies that you use to deal with them.

SITUATION	DIALECTICAL TENSION	STRATEGY FOR MANAGING
EXAMPLE: *Sandra, nineteen, and her mother, Tracy, have become good friends over the past few years. Sandra now has a serious boyfriend and spends less time talking to her mother.*	*The open-privacy dialectic is probably at work here. Sandra and Tracy continue to share the intimacy of their mother-daughter relationship, but privacy needs about the boyfriend probably keep them at more distance.*	*Sandra and Tracy are likely to use the segmentation strategy, in which they maintain openness about many areas but keep certain areas of the boyfriend relationship "off limits."*
1. Daryl is new to the software firm where Steve has been for five years. Daryl has asked Steve to play golf this weekend. Steve is uncomfortable about mixing business and pleasure, but still wants to have a good working relationship with Daryl.		
2. Nesto and Gina have been dating for six months. They continue to enjoy one another's company, but each has begun to notice annoying little habits that the other one has.		

SITUATION	DIALECTICAL TENSION	STRATEGY FOR MANAGING
3. Jenner and A. J. are siblings who have always relied on one another completely. Jenner appreciates A. J.'s dependability, but wishes their times together weren't so boring.		
4. Eugenia and Shane have worked at the same business for twenty years. They have collaborated on a number of projects. They've tried to get together socially, but their spouses don't seem to get along.		
5. Christina and Nicole are roommates. Christina wants them to share everything, but Nicole is not proud of a few things she's done and doesn't want to face her friend's judgment.		
6. Richard and Matt have been best friends for over ten years. Richard met a woman over a year ago and married her last month. Both Richard and Matt are trying to work out their "new" relationship.		
7. Your example:		
8. Your example:		

8.2 RELATIONAL STAGES
Activity Type: Skill Builder, Invitation to Insight

PURPOSES

1. To identify stages of relational development.
2. To classify stages of relational development.
3. To synthesize theory (text passages) with examples.

INSTRUCTIONS

1.   Discuss the various situations listed below.
2.   Identify the relational stage(s) that may these behaviors illustrate (e.g., initiating, experimenting, intensifying, integrating, bonding, differentiating, circumscribing, avoiding, stagnating, terminating).
3.   Cite a brief passage from Chapter 8 that verifies the stage of the relationship.
4.   Record relational situations of your own in the same manner.

EXAMPLE

Two friends are discussing the effects of divorce in their families.
Relational stage illustrated *This type of self-disclosure would most likely occur in an intensifying stage of a relationship, where the friends have gone beyond the small talk of experimenting and are beginning to develop more trust, more depth rather than breadth of self-disclosure, and where secrets are told and favors given.*

1. Two friends are telling one another about using/refusing drugs.

    Relational stage illustrated _____
    Cite a brief passage to verify the stage of the relationship

    _____

    _____

    _____

2.   Two classmates are comparing the results of their first exam.

    Relational stage illustrated _____

    Cite a brief passage to verify the stage of the relationship

    _____

    _____

    _____

3. Two people seated next to each other on an overseas flight begin telling one another about their past romantic involvements.

    Relational stage illustrated _____

Cite a brief passage to verify the stage of the relationship

_____

_____

_____

_____

4. Two long-term friends are discussing their worries and feelings of responsibility regarding their parents' advancing age.

Relational stage illustrated _____

Cite a brief passage to verify the stage of the relationship

_____

_____

_____

5. Cousins who practically lived at each other's homes as teenagers five years ago, now seem to have nothing to talk about.

Relational stage illustrated _____

Cite a brief passage to verify the stage of the relationship

_____

_____

_____

6. A divorced couple meets briefly to discuss education and vacation plans for their children.

Relational stage illustrated _____

Cite a brief passage to verify the stage of the relationship

_____

_____

_____

7. A man and woman who dated for six months during college ten years ago now find themselves working for the same company.

Relational stage illustrated _____

Cite a brief passage to verify the stage of the relationship

_____

_____

_____

8. A manager and employee have agreed to sit down and talk about the problems they are experiencing with each other.

Relational stage illustrated _____

Cite a brief passage to verify the stage of the relationship

_____

_____

_____

9. Your example: _____

Relational stage illustrated _____

Cite a brief passage to verify the stage of the relationship

_____

_____

_____

10. Your example: _____

Relational stage illustrated _____

Cite a brief passage to verify the stage of the relationship

_____

_____

_____

8.3 REPAIRING DAMAGED RELATIONSHIPS

Activity Type: Invitation to Insight

PURPOSES

1. To identify types of transgressions in relationships.
2. To classify transgressions in relationships according to two different schemes.
3. To evaluate the effectiveness of various strategies for repair.

INSTRUCTIONS

1. Consider the various situations listed below.
2. Identify the type of transgression for each set of categories (columns two and three) and give your reasons for classify it as you do.
3. Evaluate the options for repair along with the reasons you'd make the choice you do.
4. Record and analyze relational situations from your experience, your observations, films or books.

Designer: The first and last columns should be wider than the middle two. The two in the middle only require students to write one word, so they can be slimmer.

SITUATION	TYPE OF TRANSGRESSION FROM 8.1 P. 286 No commitment Distance Disrespect Problematic emotion Aggression	TYPE OF RELATIONAL TRANSGRESSION Minor/significant Social/relational Deliberate/ unintentional One-time/incremental	STRATEGIES FOR RELATIONAL REPAIR acknowledgement apology compensation Others:
1. Your sibling works for the same company you do. You were applying for a promotion and really wanted the job. Unknown to you, your sibling also applied and got the job.			
2. You and your (friend/partner/roo mmate—you choose) make plans to travel to Mexico together next summer. Each of you agrees to ask for			

the same weeks of vacation and sign up for the same flights. You request your time off, pay for your flights, and mentally prepare for the trip. Five weeks before the trip, the other person tells you he/she has decided not to "waste" a week of vacation in Mexico.			

8.4 RECOGNIZING RELATIONAL MESSAGES

Activity Type: Skill Builder

PURPOSES

1. To illustrate that virtually every message has content and relational dimensions.
2. To classify the relational dimensions of common messages.

INSTRUCTIONS

1. Read each message below. Picture in your mind the nonverbal behaviors that accompany each of the statements.
2. Describe the relational issues that seem to be involved in each of the situations. Use your text to *label and explain* the relational dimensions of **affinity, immediacy, respect and control** shown by the speaker in each example.
3. In numbers 16-18, record the content of messages you have sent and identify the relational levels involved.

MESSAGE CONTENT	RELATIONAL DIMENSION (affinity, immediacy, respect, control)
Example: You tell your romantic partner, " . . . Anyhow, that's what I think. What do you think?"	*High in immediacy because I invite involvement and show interest by my tone.* *High in affinity as I show liking by my eye contact and touch.*
Example: Your instructor invites the class to, "Tell me what's working and what isn't."	*Low in control as the instructor invites influence over how the course is run.* *High in respect by valuing the opinions of students.*
1. You ask a friend to come over and the reply is, "I'm sorry, but I have to work."	
2. Someone you live with complains, "You don't help out enough around the house."	
3. Your roommate says, "You're no fun. I think I'm going to bed."	
4. Your boss asks, "Are your hours working out?"	
5. Your boss says, "You'll need a doctor's note to verify your illness."	
6. Your friend teases, "You can't seem to remember the important stuff."	

7. Your parent says, "I know you'll make the right decision."	
8. Your romantic partner says, "I need you to let me know where you are."	
9. Someone reminds you, "Drive carefully."	
10. A family member says you should spend more time at home and you reply, "I'll do what I please."	
11. The doctor's receptionist says, "Can you hold, please?" when you call to make an appointment.	
12. You are getting ready to leave and your partner says, "You're going to wear *that*?"	
13. A friend says, "Fine" and hangs up the phone.	
14. When you ask if you can take time off, your boss rolls eyes and sighs, "Again?"	
15. You tell your friend you don't feel well, and the response is, "Had too good a time last night?"	
Now, record the **content** of messages you've sent in this column.	Identify the **relational dimensions** of those messages in this column.
16.	
17.	
18.	

8.5 MEDIATED MESSAGES – RELATIONAL DYNAMICS
Activity Type: Group Discussion

PURPOSE

To analyze relational dynamics in mediated contexts.

INSTRUCTIONS

Discuss each of the questions below in your group. Prepare written answers for your instructor, or be prepared to contribute to a large group discussion, comparing your experiences with those of others in your class.

1. Identify how mediated forms of communication are advantageous or disadvantageous during the coming together stages of relationships

_____

_____

_____

_____

2. Relationships require maintenance. Discuss how various types of mediated communication might be employed for each of these methods of maintaining relationships: positivity, openness, assurances, social networks, sharing tasks.

_____

_____

_____

3. Does the widespread use of mediated forms of communication make it easier or harder to initiate relationships? Explain.

_____

_____

_____

4. How are relational messages of respect and immediacy conveyed in e-mail? In text messages? In voice messages?

_____

_____

8.6 YOUR CALL—RELATIONAL DYNAMICS
Activity Type: Group Discussion

PURPOSE

To analyze the role of self-disclosure in a relationship.

INSTRUCTIONS

Use the case below and the discussion questions that follow to discuss the variety of communication issues involved in effective communication. Make notes on this page, add other pages on your own, or prepare a group report/analysis based on your discussion. Add your own experiences to individualize the analysis to make it **Your Call**.

CASE

Since moving into her apartment Maria feels neglected by her mom. Maria says, "She seldom calls me since I've been away at college. She's so busy doing her yoga and car-pooling for my younger brother that she always sounds rushed when I call. I want to let her know that I want her to make more of an effort to call me and visit me without sounding needy or like I can't take care of myself. I have my own life away from her, but I want to maintain the close relationship we've always had."

1. Identify the stage of this relationship. Use a quotation from *Looking Out, Looking In* to support

   your choice.

   _____

   _____

2. Explain any dialectical tensions you can identify in this relationship.

   _____

   _____

3. Evaluate the various ways of dealing with the dialectical tensions. Which do you think would be most satisfying in this situation? Why?

   _____

   _____

4. Which of these methods of maintaining relationships would be most useful for Maria and her mom: positivity, openness, assurances, social networks, or sharing tasks? For each, give a concrete example of what Maria or her mom could do.

   _____

   _____

   _____

   _____

STUDY GUIDE
CHECK YOUR UNDERSTANDING

TRUE/FALSE

Mark the statements below as true or false. Correct statements that are false on the lines below to create a true statement.

_____ 1. Communication in all cultures has both task and relational dimensions.

_____

_____ 2. Acknowledgement and apology are two ways of repairing relationships.

_____

_____ 3. Forgiveness usually increases emotional distress and aggression.

_____

_____ 4. Lack of eye contact and increased distance from someone are ways to communicate immediacy.

_____

_____ 5. Respect and affinity are identical relational messages.

_____

_____ 6. The struggle to achieve important, but seemingly incompatible goals in relationships, results in the creation of dialectical tension.

_____

_____ 7. The struggle between independence and dependence in a relationship is called the openness-privacy dialectic.

_____

_____ 8. "I like the way we don't discuss our political differences in public." is an example of metacommunicaton.

_____

_____ 9. We are rarely attracted to people who are different from us.

_____

_____ 10. Relational partners often go through evolving cycles in which they can repeat a relational stage at a new level.

_____

COMPLETION

Fill in the blanks below with the correct terms chosen from the list below.

Dialectical   Positivity   relational transgression
openness   attraction variable   metacommunication
forgiveness   immediacy   appearance
complementarity

1. _____ The messages people exchange about their communication; communication about communication.

2. _____ a relational maintenance strategy of keeping the relational climate upbeat and avoiding disapproval or unconstructive remarks.

3. _____ A strategy to maintain a relationship that involves talking directly about relationship and disclosing needs and concerns

4. _____ is an explanation for what makes us want to develop personal relationships with some people and not with others.

5. _____ a violation of the explicit or implicit terms of the relationship

6. _____ a method of relational repair that promotes physical and emotional health

7. _____ an attraction variable that is most important at the beginning of relationships, and less important over time.

8. _____ an attraction variable in which people are different in ways that meet each of their needs.

9. _____ a relational message that conveys involvement and interest

10. _____ is a tension that arises when two incompatible goals exist in a relationship.

MULTIPLE CHOICE

Place the letter of the developmental stage of the relationship on the line before its example found below.

a. initiating   f. differentiating
b. experimenting   g. circumscribing
c. intensifying   h. stagnating
d. integrating   i. avoiding
e. bonding   j. terminating

_____ 1. A public ritual marks this stage.

_____ 2. First glances and "sizing up" each other typifies this stage.

_____ 3. Called the "we" stage, this stage involves increasing self-disclosure.

_____ 4. Lots of "small talk" typifies this stage.

_____ 5. This stage involves much focus on individual rather than dyadic interests.

_____ 6. There's very little growth or experimentation in this stage.

_____ 7. This stage involves much behavior that talks around the relational issues because the partners expect bad feelings.

_____ 8. The partners' social circles merge at this stage and they make purchases or commitments together.

_____ 9. No attempts are made to contact the other at this stage.

_____ 10. The relationship is redefined or dissolved at this stage.

_____ 11. A marriage ceremony would be typical here.

_____ 12. Roommates who make sure they are never in the same room and who are tolerating one another only until the lease is up might be at this stage.

_____ 13. A couple who avoids talking about future commitment because they are afraid of how the discussion will go is probably at this state.

_____ 14. This stage represents most communication at a social gathering where people are just getting to know one another.

_____ 15. In this stage, people spend an increasing amount of time together, asking for support from one another and doing favors for one another.

CHAPTER 8 STUDY GUIDE ANSWERS

TRUE/FALSE

1. T	4. F	7. F	10. T
2. T	5. F	8. T	
3. F	6. T	9. F	

COMPLETION

1. metacommunication	5. relational transgression	9. IMMEDIACY
2. Positivity	6. forgiveness	10. dialectical
3. OPENNESS	7. appearance	
4. attraction variable	8. complementarity	

MULTIPLE CHOICE

1. e	4. b	7. g	10. j	13. g
2. a	5. f	8. d	11. e	14. b
3. c	6. h	9. i	12. i	15. c

CHAPTER NINE

Intimacy and Distance in Relational Communication

OUTLINE

Use this outline to take notes as you read the chapter in the text or as your instructor lectures in class.

I. **INTIMACY IN RELATIONSHIPS**
  A. **The dimensions of intimacy**
    1.. Physical
    2. Intellectual
    3. Emotional
    4. Shared activities
  B. **Masculine and feminine intimacy styles**
    1. Value placed on talk or activity
    2. Gender role not biological sex influences
  C. **Cultural influences on intimacy**
    1. Historical
    2. National cultures
      a. individualist
      b. collectivist
    3. Co-cultures and class

  D. **Intimacy in Computer-Mediated Communication**
    1. speed
    2. choices
  E. **Limits of Intimacy**
    1. time and energy
    2. satisfaction

II. **SELF-DISCLOSURE IN RELATIONSHIPS**
  A. **Definition**
    1. Deliberate, significant, unknown by others
    2. usually in dyads, incremental, scarce, context

B. **Degrees of Self-Disclosure**
   1. Social penetration model: Breadth and depth
   2. Clichés, facts, opinions, feelings

C. **A Model of Self-Disclosure: Johari Window**
   1. Open
   2. Hidden
   3. Blind
   4. Unknown

D. **Benefits and Risks of Self-Disclosure**
   1. Benefits
      a. Catharsis
      b. Reciprocity
      c. Self-clarification
      d..Self-validation
      e. Identity management
      f. Relational maintenance
      g. Social influence
   2. Risks
      a. Rejection
      b. Negative impression
      c. Decrease in relational satisfaction
      d. Loss of influence
      e. Hurting the other person

E. **Guidelines for Self-Disclosure**
   1. Moral obligation
   2. Importance of the other to you
   3. Appropriate amount and type
   4. Risk
   5. Relevance
   6. Constructive effects
   7. Clear and understandable
   8. Reciprocation

III. **ALTERNATIVES TO SELF-DISCLOSURE**

   A. **Silence**

   B. **Lying**
      1. Benevolent lies
      2. Reasons for lying
         a. Save face
         b. Avoid tension/conflict
         c. Guide social interaction
         d. Expand/reduce relationships
         e. Gain power
      3. Effects of lies - threats to the relationship

   C. **Equivocating**
      1. Spares embarrassment
      2. Saves face
      3. Provides an alternative to lying

D. Hinting
1. May prevent receiver or sender embarrassment
2. Hints may not be perceived

E. The Ethics of Evasion
1. Manage difficult situations
2. motives and effect
1. lies may be unchallenged if they
    a. are expected
    b. are mutually advantageous
    c. avoid embarrassment
    d. avoid unpleasant truths
    e. were requested

KEY TERMS

benevolent lie
breadth
clichés
depth
intimacy
Johari Window
self-disclosure
social penetration

ACTIVITIES

9.1 BREADTH AND DEPTH OF RELATIONSHIPS

Activity Type: Invitation to Insight

PURPOSES

1. To help you understand the breadth and depth of a relationship that is important to you.
2. To help you decide if you are satisfied with the breadth and depth of that relationship, and possibly to modify it.

INSTRUCTIONS

1. Use the form below to make a social penetration model for a significant relationship you have, indicating the depth and breadth of various areas. See Figure 9.1 and 9.2 in Chapter 9of *Looking Out/Looking In* for an example of the social penetration model.
2. Answer the questions at the end of the exercise.

DESIGNER: LABEL THIS 9.1

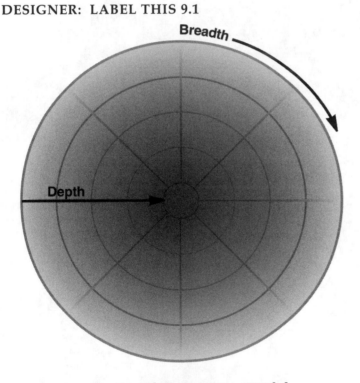

FIGURE 8-5   **Social Penetration Model**

Significant relationship described: _____

CONCLUSIONS

How deep or shallow is your relationship with this person?

_____

_____

Does the depth vary from one area (breadth) to another? In what way?

_____

_____

_____

Are you satisfied with the depth and breadth of this relationship? Why or why not?

_____

_____

_____

If you are not satisfied, what could you do to change the relationship?   What would you predict the results would be?

_____

_____

_____

_____

_____

_____

_____

_____

9.2 REASONS FOR NONDISCLOSURE

Activity Type: Invitation to Insight

PURPOSE

To give you an idea of the reasons you do not disclose and the rationality of these reasons.

INSTRUCTIONS

1. Choose a particular individual about whom you want to analyze your self-disclosing behavior.
2. In the column to the left of each item, indicate the extent to which you use each reason to avoid disclosing.

   5 = almost always   2 = rarely
   4 = often   1 = never
   3 = sometimes

3. In the column to the right of each item, indicate how reasonable and realistic the reason is.

   5 = totally realistic
   4 = mostly realistic
   3 = partly realistic, partly unrealistic
   2 = mostly unrealistic
   1 = totally unrealistic

**How Frequently
Do You Use
the Reason?**

**How Realistic
and Rational
Is the Reason?**

_____ 1. I can't find the opportunity to self-disclose with this person. _____

_____ 2. If I disclose I might hurt the other person. _____

_____ 3. If I disclose I might be evaluating or judging the person. _____

_____ 4. I can't think of topics that I would disclose. _____

_____ 5. Self-disclosure would give information that might be used against me at some time. _____

_____ 6. If I disclose it might cause me to make personal changes. _____

_____ 7. Self-disclosure might threaten relationships I have with people other than the close acquaintance to whom I disclose. _____

_____ 8. Self-disclosure is a sign of weakness.

_____ 9. If I disclose I might lose control over the other person. _____

_____ 10. If I disclose I might discover I am less than I wish to be. _____

*Based on a survey developed by Lawrence B. Rosenfeld, "Self-Disclosure Avoidance: Why Am I Afraid to Tell You Who I Am?" *Communication Monographs* 46 (1979): 63–74.

How Frequently Do You Use the Reason?		How Realistic and Rational Is the Reason?
_____	11. If I disclose I might project an image I do not want to project.	_____
_____	12. If I disclose the other person might not understand what I was saying.	_____
_____	13. If I disclose the other person might evaluate me negatively.	_____
_____	14. Self-disclosure is a sign of some emotional disturbance.	_____
_____	15. Self-disclosure might hurt our relationship.	_____
_____	16. I am afraid that self-disclosure might lead to an intimate relationship with the other person.	_____
_____	17. Self-disclosure might threaten my physical safety.	_____
_____	18. If I disclose I might give information that makes me appear inconsistent.	_____
_____	19. Any other reasons: _____	_____

What does this personal survey tell you about your thoughts and feelings about self-disclosure with this person?

_____

_____

_____

Do you think your level of self-disclosure is appropriate or inappropriate with this person? Why or why not?

_____

_____

How would you summarize and categorize the major reasons that you self-disclose using these categories: Catharsis, Reciprocity, Self-clarification, Self-validation, Identity management, Relational maintenance, Social influence?

_____

_____

_____

How different would your survey look if you'd chosen a different relationship? Why?

_____

_____

9.3 DEGREES OF SELF-DISCLOSURE

Activity Type: Invitation to Insight

PURPOSES

1. To demonstrate that self-disclosure can operate on a variety of levels, some quite intimate and others less revealing.
2. To analyze various types of self-disclosure.

INSTRUCTIONS

For each of the following topics, write two statements for each level of self-disclosure. (See Chapter 9 of *Looking Out/Looking In* for descriptions of each level.)

EXAMPLE

Topic: School

1. Clichés
   a. *Finals are no fun!*
   b. *Textbooks sure are expensive!*
2. Facts
   a. *I'm a psychology major at the university.*
   b. *I'm getting a teaching certificate so I'll be able to teach social studies.*
3. Opinions
   a. *I think people over 18 should be allowed to keep a driver's license if they don't vote..*
   b. *I don't think instructors should count attendance as part of a person's grade.*

4. Feelings
   a. *I feel scared when I think about the future. I'm almost finished with four years of college, and I'm still confused about what to do with my life.*
   b. *I get angry when Professor Autel doesn't prepare adequately for our class.*

TOPIC: MY FAMILY

1. Clichés

    a. _____

    b. _____

2. Facts

    a. _____

    b. _____

3. Opinions

    a. _____

    b. _____

4. Feelings

    a. _____

    b. _____

TOPIC: MY CAREER PLANS

1. Clichés

    a. _____

    b. _____

2. Facts

    a. _____

    b. _____

3. Opinions

    a. _____

    b. _____

4. Feelings

    a. _____

    b. _____

TOPIC: POLITICS

1. Clichés

    a. _____

    b. _____

2. Facts

    a. _____

    b. _____

3. Opinions

    a. _____

    b. _____

4. Feelings

    a. _____

    b. _____

TOPIC: SPORTS

1. Clichés

    a. _____

    b. _____

2. Facts

    a. _____

    b. _____

3. Opinions

    a. _____

    b. _____

4. Feelings

    a. _____

    b. _____

9.4 DISCLOSURE AND ALTERNATIVES

Activity Type: Skill Builder

PURPOSES

1.   To generate responses to relational situations.
2.   To evaluate the effectiveness and ethics of each situation.

INSTRUCTIONS

1.   For each situations described below, record responses for the types listed.
2.   Evaluate the effectiveness and ethics of your responses.
3.   Describe a disclosure situation of your own in the same manner.

EXAMPLE

Your friend asks you if you had a good time when you went out with his cousin last night.
Self-disclosure *I didn't have a great time, but then we were just getting to know one another. I don't think that we had much in common.*
Silence: *If I don't answer or don't say anything, my friend might think it was worse than I do.*
Lying: *Your cousin was a lot of fun and the movie was great.*
Equivocating. *First dates are really times of discovery, aren't they?*
Hinting: *I don't think I have to have a great time every night.*
Which response is most effective/which most ethical? *I think equivocating is effective.*
While I wasn't exactly self-disclosing with my friend, I just don't want to tell him how boring I think his cousin is. I haven't lied and they both of them can save face, too.

1.   After your romantic partner has a bad week at work, his/her boss asks you how he/she is feeling about the company.

Self-Disclosure _____

Silence_____

Lying_____

Equivocating _____

Hinting _____

Which responses are most effective/which most ethical? _____

_____

_____

2.   You are applying to rent an apartment that prohibits animals. You have a cat.

Self-Disclosure _____

Silence_____

Lying_____

Equivocating _____

Hinting _____

Which responses are most effective/which most ethical? _____

_____

_____

3. Your siblings ask you about your financial status (which is much better than theirs).

Self-Disclosure _____

Silence _____

Lying _____

Equivocating _____

Hinting _____

Which responses are most effective/which most ethical? _____

_____

_____

4. Your roommates ask what you think of the bright posters they've just put up around the living room.

Self-Disclosure _____

Silence _____

Lying _____

Equivocating _____

Hinting _____

Which responses are most effective/which most ethical? _____

_____

_____

5. Your romantic partner asks how many other people you've really loved before you met him or her.

Self-Disclosure _____

Silence _____

Lying _____

Equivocating _____

Hinting _____

Which responses are most effective/which most ethical? _____

_____

_____

6. Your very opinionated father, whose opinions differ from yours, asks what you think of the person running for governor.

Self-Disclosure _____

Silence _____

Lying_____

Equivocating _____

Hinting _____

Which responses are most effective/which most ethical? _____

_____

_____

7. Your boss wants to know what your plans for the future are; you're looking around.

Self-Disclosure _____

Silence _____

Lying_____

Equivocating _____

Hinting _____

Which responses are most effective/which most ethical? _____

_____

_____

8. Your mother asks you about what your brother has been up to lately. You know he is probably moving out of state in a few months but he doesn't want your mom to know yet.

Self-Disclosure _____

Silence _____

Lying_____

Equivocating _____

Hinting _____

Which responses are most effective/which most ethical? _____

_____

_____

9. Your example: _____

Self-Disclosure _____

Silence _____

Lying _____

Equivocating _____

Hinting _____

Which responses are most effective/which most ethical? _____

_____

9.5 MEDIATED MESSAGES – RELATIONAL DYNAMICS
Activity Type: Group Discussion

PURPOSE

To analyze relational dynamics in mediated contexts.

INSTRUCTIONS

Discuss each of the questions below in your group.

1. Describe how self-disclosure might occur **differently** in mediated contexts (letters, e-mail, telephone, instant messaging/chat, online courses) than in face-to-face communication.

    _____

    _____

    _____

    _____

2. Do you think self-disclosure occurs more **often** face-to-face or in specific mediated contexts?

    _____

    _____

    _____

3. When people want to self-disclose for catharsis, why might it be more difficult in certain

    mediated channels ? Why might it be easier in certain mediated channels ?

    _____

    _____

4. Can satisfying relationships be maintained without face-to-face communication?

    _____

    _____

5. Which type(s) of intimacy (physical, intellectual, emotional, shared activities) are more apt to develop in mediated contexts than face-to-face? Why?

    _____

    _____

    _____

    _____

9.6 YOUR CALL—RELATIONAL DYNAMICS
Activity Type: Group Discussion

PURPOSE

To analyze the role of self-disclosure in a relationship.

INSTRUCTIONS

Use the case below and the discussion questions that follow to discuss the variety of communication issues involved in effective communication. Make notes on this page, add other pages on your own, or prepare a group report/analysis based on your discussion. Add your own experiences to individualize the analysis to make it **Your Call**.

CASE

Leilani and Malcolm dated one another exclusively for three years. They broke up for six months, and now are back together and talking about getting married. While they were broken up, Leilani became intimate with a casual friend of Malcolm's for a brief time before she realized that she really loved only Malcolm. During this same time period, Malcolm dated around; he was attracted to a number of women, but he did not get serious about any one. Malcolm has now told Leilani that he believes they should tell one another everything about the time they were apart.

1. Do you think full self-disclosure is important in this relationship? Why or why not?

   _____

   _____

2. Use other relationships (your own and others) to evaluate how important full self-disclosure is to committed relationships. Cite times when full disclosure may be more harmful than helpful?

   _____

   _____

3. Evaluate the alternatives to self-disclosure in this situation. Explain how lies, benevolent lies, partial disclosure, equivocation or hinting might be more effective than full disclosure?

   _____

   _____

4. Using quotations from the text, evaluate how much Leilani and Malcolm should disclose to each other about the six months they were apart.

   _____

   _____

STUDY GUIDE

CHECK YOUR UNDERSTANDING

CROSSWORD PUZZLE

ACROSS

2. the second level of disclosure that discloses information about the self
3. first dimension of self-disclosure involving the range of subjects being discussed
7. a state of personal sharing arising from physical, intellectual, or emotional contact
9. the process of deliberately revealing information about oneself that is significant and that would not normally be known by others is self-_____
11. Engaging another person in an _____ of important, exciting, and powerful ideas can lead to intellectual intimacy.
15. confirmation of a belief you hold about yourself is self-_____

16. a social _____ model that describes relationships in terms of their breadth and depth

DOWN

1. disclosing information in an attempt to "get it off your chest"
4. using ambiguous language that has two or more equally plausible meanings
5. a dimension of self-disclosure involving a shift from relatively nonrevealing messages to more personal ones
6. giving subtle clues to get a desired response from others without direct stating it
8. an act of self-disclosure calculated in advance to achieve a desired result
10. a motivation for self-disclosing based on the research evidence that individuals disclosing information about themselves encourage others to self-disclose in return
12. a motivation for self-disclosing based on creating relational success by increasing honesty and depth of sharing
13. cliché conversation is similar to what is commonly called _____ talk
14. a model that describes the relationship between self-disclosure and self-awareness is the _____ Window

TRUE/FALSE

Mark the statements below as true or false. Correct statements that are false on the lines below to create a true statement.

_____ 1. Intimacy is definitely rewarding, so maximizing intimacy is the best way of relating to others.

_____

_____ 2. An obsession with intimacy can actually lead to less satisfying relationships.

_____

_____ 3. Research shows that male-male relationships involve less disclosure than male-female or female-female relationships.

_____

_____ 4. In some situations, persons have a moral and ethical imperative to self-disclose.

_____

_____ 5. Germans and Japanese are more disclosing than members of any culture studied.

_____

_____ 6. In some collectivistic cultures, there is a great difference between the way people communicate with members of their "in-groups" and with their "out-groups."

_____

_____ 7. In a casual relationship, the depth of self-disclosure may be great, but not the breadth.

_____

_____   8.   Self-disclosure usually leads to reciprocity.

_____

_____   9.   Self-disclosure is by nature, negative, not positive information.

_____

_____   10. People justify over half of their lies as ways to avoid embarrassment for themselves or others.

_____

COMPLETION

Fill in the blanks below with the correct terms chosen from the list below.

open	hidden	blind	unknown	intellectual
physical	emotional	benevolent	hinting	

1. _____ is the type of intimacy that comes from an exchange of important ideas.

2. _____ is the type of intimacy that comes from touching, struggling, or sex.

3. _____ is the type of intimacy that comes from exchanging important feelings.

4. _____ is an explanation for what makes us want to develop personal relationships with some people and not with others.

5. _____ is a type of lie that is intended to help, not harm others.

6. _____ is a frame of the Johari Window that consists of information that you know about yourself but aren't willing to reveal to others.

7. _____ is a frame of the Johari Window that consists of information of which neither you nor the other person is aware.

8. _____ is a frame of the Johari Window that consists of information of which both you and the other person are aware.

9. _____ is a frame of the Johari Window that consists of information of which you are unaware but the other person in the relationship knows.

10. _____ is an alternative to self-disclosure in which the person gives only a clue to the direct meaning of the response.

MULTIPLE CHOICE

1. Which of these is not a dimension of intimacy in interpersonal relationships
   a. physical
   b. shared activities
   c. chronological
   d. emotional

2. Researchers have found that, with regard to intimacy and CMC
   a. intimacy can occur in computer-mediated communication
   b. intimacy rarely occurs in computer-mediated communication
   c. computers are useful for developing but not maintaining relationships
   d. CMC is superior to face-to-face interaction

3. Self-disclosure, by definition, is all of these except
   a. intentional
   b. significant
   c. not known by others
   d. accidental

4. According to the social penetration model, two dimensions of self-disclosure are
   a. breadth and depth
   b. reciprocal and positive
   c. open and hidden
   d. hinting and equivocating

5. According to the social penetration model, which level of conversation involves the greatest risk
   a. fact
   b. feelings
   c. opinions
   d. clichés

6. The Johari Window model illustrates
   a. ethical responses
   b. self-disclosure
   c. risks
   d. intimidation responses

7. Your text identifies all of these reasons that people self-disclose except
   a. catharsis
   b. reciprocity
   c. job satisfaction
   d. self-clarification

8. Self-validation, identity management, and relationship maintenance have been identified as reasons why people
   a. self-disclose
   b. reject intimacy
   c. create relationships
   d. create relational tensions

9. Among the risks of self-disclosure are all of these except the possibility of
   a. less relational satisfaction

     b. rejection
     c. creating a negative impression
     d. a relationship with only CMC

10. Self-disclosure
     a. usually occurs in large groups
     b. usually occurs incrementally
     c. is generally coerced, not voluntary
     d. is the only ethical response in most situations

CHAPTER 9 STUDY GUIDE ANSWERS

CROSSWORD PUZZLE

The completed crossword contains the following answers:

- 1 (down) catharsis
- 2 (across) facts
- 3 (across) breadth
- 4 (down) equiving / equiv...
- 5 (down) depth
- 6 (down) hinting
- 7 (across) intimacy
- 8 (down) manipulation
- 9 (across) disclosure
- 10 (down) reciprocity
- 11 (across) exchange
- 12 (down) enhancement
- 13 (down) small
- 14 (down) Johari
- 15 (across) validation
- 16 (across/down) penetration
- 17 (across) staircase

TRUE/FALSE

1. F	4. T	7. F	10. T
2. T	5. F	8. T	
3. T	6. T	9. F	

COMPLETION

1. intellectual
2. physical
3. emotional
4. silence

5. benevolent
6. hidden
7. unknown
8. open

9. blind
10. hinting

MULTIPLE CHOICE

1. c
2. a
3. d

4. a
5. b
6. b

7. c
8. a
9. d

10. b

C H A P T E R T E N

Improving Communication Climates

OUTLINE

Use this outline to take notes as you read the chapter in the text and/or as your instructor lectures in class.

I. **COMMUNICATION CLIMATE: THE KEY TO POSITIVE RELATIONSHIPS**
   A. **Confirming and Disconfirming Communication**
      1. Types of confirming messages
         a. Recognition
         b. Acknowledgement
         c. Endorsement

      2. Types of disconfirming messages
         a. Impervious responses
         b. Verbal abuse
         c. Generalized complaining
         d. Interrupting
         e. Irrelevant responses
         f. Tangential responses
         g. Impersonal responses
         h. Ambiguous responses
         i. Incongruous responses
   B. **How Communication Climates Develop**
      1. Escalatory conflict spirals
      2. De-escalatory conflict spirals

II. **DEFENSIVENESS: CAUSES AND REMEDIES**
   A. **Causes: Face-Threatening Acts**
   B. **Types of Defensive Reactions**
      1. Attacking the critic
         a. Verbal aggression
         b. Sarcasm
      2. Distorting critical information
         a. Rationalization
         b. Compensation
         c. Regression
      3. Avoiding dissonant information
         a. Physical avoidance
         b. Repression
         c. Apathy

        d. Displacement

C. Preventing Defensiveness in Others
1. Evaluation versus description
2. Control versus problem orientation
3. Strategy versus spontaneity
4. Neutrality versus empathy
5. Superiority versus equality
6. Certainty versus provisionalism

III. SAVING FACE: THE CLEAR MESSAGE FORMAT

A. Behavior
1. behavioral description
2. objective, factual

B. Interpretation
1. based on experience, assumptions
2. subjective

C. Feeling

D. Consequence
1. What happens to you, the speaker
2. What happens to the person you're addressing
3. What happens to others

E. Intention
1. Where you stand on an issue
2. Requests of others
3. How you plan to act in the future

F. Using the Clear Message Format
1. Order may vary
2. Use personal style
3. Combine elements
4. Take your time

IV. RESPONDING NONDEFENSIVELY TO CRITICISM

A. Seek more information
1. Ask for specifics
2. Guess about specifics
3. Paraphrase the speaker's ideas
4. Ask what the critic wants
5. Ask about the consequences
6. Ask if anything else is wrong

B. Agree with the critic
1. Agree with the facts
2. Agree with the critic's perception

KEY TERMS

ambiguous response

apathy

assertive

behavioral description

certainty

cognitive dissonance

communication climate

compensation

confirming communication

consequence statement

controlling communication

de-escalatory conflict spiral

defense mechanism

defensiveness

description

disconfirming communication

displacement

empathy

equality

escalatory conflict spiral

evaluation

face-threatening act

feeling statement

generalized complaining

Gibb categories

impersonal response

impervious response

incongruous response

intention statement

interpretation statement

interrupting response

irrelevant response

neutrality

physical avoidance

problem orientation

provisionalism

rationalization

regression

repression

sarcasm

spiral

spontaneity

strategy

superiority

tangential response

verbal abuse

verbal aggression

ACTIVITIES

10.1 UNDERSTANDING DEFENSIVE RESPONSES

Activity Type: Invitation to Insight

PURPOSE

To identify typical defensive responses and their consequences.

INSTRUCTIONS

1. Identify the person or people who would be most likely to deliver each of the following critical messages to you. If you are unlikely to hear one or more of the following messages, substitute a defensiveness-arousing topic of your own.
2. For each situation, describe
   a. the person likely to deliver the message.
   b. the typical content of the message.
   c. the general type of response(s) you make: attacking, distorting, or avoiding.
   d. your typical verbal response(s).
   e. your typical nonverbal response(s).
   f. the part of your presenting self being defended.
   g. the probable consequences of these response(s).

EXAMPLE

A negative comment about your use of time.
Person likely to deliver this message *my parents*
Typical content of the message *wasting my time watching TV instead of studying*
General type(s) of response *attacking, distorting*
Your typical verbal response(s) *"Get off my back! I work hard! I need time to relax." "I'll study later; I've got plenty of time."*
Your typical nonverbal response(s) *harsh tone of voice, sullen silence for an hour or two*
Part of presenting self being defended *good student, not lazy*
Probable consequences of your response(s) *uncomfortable silence, more criticism from parents in the future*

1. Negative comment about your managing money.

   Person likely to deliver this message _____

   Typical content of the message _____

   _____

   General type(s) of response _____

   Your typical verbal response(s) _____

   _____

   Your typical nonverbal response(s) _____

_____

Part(s) of presenting self being defended _____

Probable consequences of your response(s) _____

_____

_____

2. Criticism about your choice of friends.

Person likely to deliver this message _____

Typical content of the message _____

_____

General type(s) of response _____

Your typical verbal response(s) _____

_____

Your typical nonverbal response(s) _____

_____

Part(s) of presenting self being defended _____

Probable consequences of your response(s) _____

_____

_____

3. Criticism of a job you've just completed.

Person likely to deliver this message _____

Typical content of the message _____

_____

General type(s) of response _____

Your typical verbal response(s) _____

_____

Your typical nonverbal response(s) _____

_____

Part(s) of presenting self being defended _____

Probable consequences of your response(s) _____

_____

_____

4. Criticism of your schoolwork.

Person likely to deliver this message _____

Typical content of the message _____

_____

General type(s) of response _____

Your typical verbal response(s) _____

_____

Your typical nonverbal response(s) _____

_____

Part(s) of presenting self being defended _____

Probable consequences of your response(s) _____

_____

_____

5. Criticism of your politics, political action or lack of political involvement.

Person likely to deliver this message _____

Typical content of the message _____

_____

General type(s) of response _____

Your typical verbal response(s) _____

_____

Your typical nonverbal response(s) _____

_____

Part(s) of presenting self being defended _____

Probable consequences of your response(s) _____

_____

_____

6. A negative comment about your exercise (or lack of it).

Person likely to deliver this message _____

Typical content of the message _____

_____

General type(s) of response _____

Your typical verbal response(s) _____

_____

Your typical nonverbal response(s) _____

_____

Part(s) of presenting self being defended _____

Probable consequences of your response(s) _____

_____

_____

10.2 DEFENSIVE AND SUPPORTIVE LANGUAGE

Activity Type: Skill Builder

PURPOSE

To recognize the difference between the Gibb categories of defensive and supportive language.

INSTRUCTIONS

1. For each of the situations below, write one statement likely to arouse defensiveness and one statement likely to promote a support climate.
2. Label the Gibb category of language that each statement represents (evaluation, description, control, problem-orientation, strategy, spontaneity, neutrality, empathy, superiority, equality, certainty, or provisionalism).

EXAMPLE

A neighbor's late-night stereo music playing is disrupting your sleep.

Defense-arousing statement *Why don't you show a little consideration and turn that damn thing down? If I hear any more noise I'm going to call the police!*

Type(s) of defensive language *evaluation, control*

Supportive statement *When I hear your stereo music late at night I can't sleep, which leaves me more and more tired. I'd like to figure out some way you can listen and I can sleep.*

Type(s) of supportive language *description, problem orientation*

1. You're an adult child who moves back in with your parents. They say they expect you to follow the "rules of the house."

   Defense-arousing statement _____

   _____

   Type(s) of defensive language _____

   Supportive statement _____

   _____

   Type(s) of supportive language _____

2. Your roommate tells you you're trying to be "somebody you're not."

   Defense-arousing statement _____

   _____

   Type(s) of defensive language _____

   Supportive statement _____

   _____

   Type(s) of supportive language _____

3. A friend asks you what you see in your new romantic partner.

   Defense-arousing statement _____

   _____

   Type(s) of defensive language _____

   Supportive statement _____

   _____

   Type(s) of supportive language _____

4. Your boss says, "You call that finished?"

   Defense-arousing statement _____

   _____

   Type(s) of defensive language _____

   Supportive statement _____

   _____

   Type(s) of supportive language _____

5. Your friend buys the same thing you did after you bragged about the deal you got.

   Defense-arousing statement _____

   _____

   Type(s) of defensive language _____

   Supportive statement _____

   _____

   Type(s) of supportive language _____

6. On many occasions a friend drops by your place without calling first. Since you often have other plans, this behavior puts you in an uncomfortable position.

   Defense-arousing statement _____

   _____

   Type(s) of defensive language _____

Supportive statement _____

_____

Type(s) of supportive language _____

7. Your roommate says, "You left the lights on *again*."

Defense-arousing statement _____

_____

Type(s) of defensive language _____

Supportive statement _____

_____

Type(s) of supportive language _____

8. Your parent praises your sibling for something without mentioning you.

Defense-arousing statement _____

_____

Type(s) of defensive language _____

Supportive statement _____

_____

Type(s) of supportive language _____

9. Your situation:_____

Defense-arousing statement _____

_____

Type(s) of defensive language _____

Supportive statement _____

_____

Type(s) of supportive language _____

10.3 WRITING CLEAR MESSAGES

Activity Type: Skill Builder

PURPOSE

To turn unclear messages into clear ones.

INSTRUCTIONS

Imagine a situation in which you might have said each of the statements below. Rewrite the messages in the clear message format, being sure to include each of the five elements described in your text.

EXAMPLE

Unclear message: "It's awful when you can't trust a friend."

Clear message:

Lena, when I gave you the keys to my house so you could borrow those clothes, I

came back and found the house unlocked. (behavior)

I figured you'd know to lock up again when you left. (interpretation)

I was worried and scared. (feeling)

I thought there was a break-in and was nervous about going in. (consequence)

I want to know if you left the house unlocked and, let you know how upset I am. (intention)

1. "Just get off my case; you're not my warden."

_____ (behavior)

_____ (interpretation)

_____ (feeling)

_____ (consequence)

_____ (intention)

2. "I wish you'd pay more attention to me."

_____ (behavior)

_____ (interpretation)

_____ (feeling)

_____ (consequence)

_____ (intention)

3. "You've sure been thoughtful lately."

_____ (behavior)

_____ (interpretation)

_____ (feeling)

_____ (consequence)

_____ (intention)

4. "You're the greatest!"

_____ (behavior)

_____ (interpretation)

_____ (feeling)

_____ (consequence)

_____ (intention)

5. "Matt, you're such a slob!"

_____ (behavior)

_____ (interpretation)

_____ (feeling)

_____ (consequence)

_____ (intention)

6. "Let's just forget it; forget I ever asked for a favor."

_____ (behavior)

_____ (interpretation)

_____ (feeling)

_____ (consequence)

_____ (intention)

Now list three significant messages that you could send to important people in your life: one **complaint, one request, and one expression of appreciation**. Write them in clear message format.

8. _____ (behavior)

_____ (interpretation)

_____ (feeling)

_____ (consequence)

_____ (intention)

9. _____ (behavior)

_____ (interpretation)

_____ (feeling)

_____ (consequence)

_____ (intention)

10. _____ (behavior)

_____ (interpretation)

_____ (feeling)

_____ (consequence)

_____ (intention)

CRITICAL THINKING:

1. Compare and contrast the perception check with the clear message.

2. You are faced with a co-worker's difficult behavior: taking credit for work that you did. Would you use a perception check? A clear message? Both? In what order? Why?

10.4 NONDEFENSIVE RESPONSES TO CRITICISM

Activity Type: Skill Builder, Group Activity

PURPOSE

To practice nondefensive responses to typical criticisms you may face.

INSTRUCTIONS

1. For each situation below, write a nondefensive response you could use that follows the guidelines of seeking more information or agreeing with the critic described in Chapter 10 of *Looking Out/Looking In.*
2. Join with two partners and identify the members as A, B, and C.
3. Role-play situations 1 and 2 with A responding to the criticisms offered by B, while C uses 10.5 *Coping with Criticism* to evaluate A's behavior.
4. Switch roles so that B responds to C's criticisms on items 3 and 4, while A completes the checklist.
5. Switch roles again so that C responds to A's criticisms on items 5 and 6, while B completes the checklist.

SITUATION/CRITICISM	EFFECTIVE RESPONSE TO CRITICISM
1. You've been late to work every day this week. Just who do you think you are that you can come wandering in after the rest of us are already working?	
2. This place is a mess! Don't you care about how we live?	
3. You should have consulted somebody before acting on that.	
4. Your brother got terrific grades this term and worked 20 hours a week	

Class_____   Name _____

SITUATION/CRITICISM	EFFECTIVE RESPONSE TO CRITICISM
5. How could you have been so thoughtless at the party last night?	
6. Why don't you ever initiate anything?	
7. You think I'm your personal servant!	
8. Haven't you finished that yet?	
9. You haven't been very productive.	
10. I wonder what those parents do to make their children so well-behaved when yours run all over the place.	
11. Criticism of you:	
12. Criticism of you:	

10.5 COPING WITH CRITICISM
Activity Type: Oral Skill

PURPOSE

To practice nondefensive responses to criticisms.

INSTRUCTIONS

1. Form triads and identify members as A, B, and C. (OR form dyads, record the following, and receive evaluation from your instructor)
2. Person A describes a common defensiveness-arousing criticism he or she faces, identifying the critic, topic, and the critic's behavior.
3. Person B paraphrases and questions A until he or she understands the critic's behavior.
4. Persons A and B then role-play the situation, with B criticizing A while A practices the eight skills of seeking more information and agreeing with the critic as described in Chapter 10 of *Looking Out/Looking In.*
5. Person C uses *Coping with Criticism* to evaluate A's skill at responding nondefensively.
6. After the role-play, person C provides feedback to person A.
7. Rotate roles and repeat steps 1–6 until both B and C have had the chance to practice responding nondefensively to criticism.
8. On a separate page, write a thoughtful, realistically complete assessment of how you used the skills for coping with criticism here, and how you could apply these skills in everyday life.

CHECKLIST

Seeks additional information to understand criticism and critic

    —asks for specific details of criticism   _____

    —guesses about specific details when critic does not supply facts   _____

    —asks what the critic wants   _____

    —asks critic to describe the consequences of behavior   _____

    ___paraphrases   _____

    —asks what else is wrong   _____

Agrees as appropriate with criticism

    —agrees with facts (truth only)

    —agrees with critic's right to perceive event differently

    ("I can understand why it looks that way to you because . . .")   _____

Vocal and nonverbal behaviors
    —indicate sincerity (voice, facial expression, posture and gestures, body orientation and distance)
    —sound realistic and consistent with speaker's style   _____

                                           Total   _____

10.6 MEDIATED MESSAGES – CLIMATE

Activity Type: Group Discussion

PURPOSE

To apply the concept of communication climate to mediated contexts.

INSTRUCTIONS

Discuss each of the questions below in your group. Prepare written answers for your instructor, or be prepared to contribute to a large group discussion, comparing your experiences with those of others in your class.

1. Describe how the use of mediated forms of communication channels (e.g., telephone, e-mail) contributes to the communication climate (emotional tone) of your relationships.

   _____

   _____

2. Compile a list of the ways we can use mediated messages to recognize, acknowledge, and endorse others.

   _____

   _____

3. Give examples of how mediated messages have contributed to or helped minimize defensive spirals (negative, ineffective patterns of communication) in your relationships.

   _____

   _____

   _____

4. Your text describes ways we can respond nondefensively to criticism. In which mediated contexts can this skill be used most effectively?

   _____

   _____

5. Go online to RateMyProfessors.com. This is an independent forum in which college students can praise—or, more often, slam—the work of their instructors. Evaluate the confirming and disconfirming aspects of this site.

   _____

   _____

   _____

10.7 YOUR CALL—CLIMATE

Activity Type: Group Discussion

PURPOSE

To analyze defensiveness in relationships.

INSTRUCTIONS

Use the case below and the discussion questions that follow to discuss the variety of communication issues involved in effective communication. Make notes on this page, add other pages on your own, or prepare a group report/analysis based on your discussion. Add your own experiences to individualize the analysis to make it **Your Call**.

CASE

Gil and Lydia are brother and sister. They love one another and feel close. Their mother often tells Gil how wonderful Lydia is to call her so often, how smart Lydia is, what a good athlete she is, and how much she enjoys Lydia bringing home her friends to visit. Mom tells Lydia how generous Gil is, how hard he works, how many interesting things he does, and how well he manages money. The overall climate of the relationship between Gil and Lydia and their mother is good, but both Gil and Lydia find themselves getting defensive when their mom spends so much time praising the other.

1. Use aspects of Gibb's theory to explain why Gil and Lydia get defensive about these positive statements about the other.

   _____

   _____

   _____

   _____

2. Discuss situations similar to the one above in which people get defensive about statements that, on the surface, are positive and supportive.

   _____

   _____

   _____

3. Write coping with criticism responses for Gil or Lydia to use the next time their mother praises their sibling.

   _____

   _____

4. How could Gil and Lydia's mother change the comments she makes about each sibling to reduce defensive reactions?

   _____

STUDY GUIDE

CHECK YOUR UNDERSTANDING

CROSSWORD PUZZLE

ACROSS

2. communication in which the sender tries to impose some sort of outcome on the receiver, usually resulting in a defensive reaction
4. a disconfirming response with more than one meaning, leaving the other party unsure of the responder's position
6. communication messages that express caring or respect for another person
8. a defense mechanism in which a person stresses a strength in one area to camouflage a shortcoming in some other area
10. communication messages that express a lack of caring or respect for another person
11. the emotional tone of a relationship between two or more individuals

12. an element of a clear message that includes future action plans and requests of others
13. a disconfirming response that is superficial or trite

DOWN

1. a defense mechanism in which a person vents hostile or aggressive feelings on a target that cannot strike back, instead of on the true target
3. a cognitive inconsistency between two conflicting pieces of information, attitudes or behavior
4. a defense mechanism in which a person avoids admitting emotional pain by pretending not to care about an event
5. a disconfirming response in which one communicator breaks into the other's communication
7. a disconfirming response that generally implies a character fault in the other person
9. a disconfirming response that ignores another person's attempt to communicate

TRUE/FALSE

Mark the statements below as true or false. Correct false statements on the lines below to create true statements.

_____   1. The tone or climate of a relationship is shaped by the degree to which the people believe themselves to be valued by one another.

_____   2. Disagreeing with another person is always disconfirming or defense-arousing.

_____   3. Most experts agree that it is psychologically healthier to have someone ignore you than disagree with you.

_____   4. Both positive and negative communication spirals have their limits; they rarely go on indefinitely.

_____   5. When the criticism leveled at us is accurate, we will not get defensive.

_____   6. Communicators strive to resolve inconsistencies or conflicting pieces of information because this "dissonant" condition is uncomfortable.

_____   7. Using Jack Gibb's supportive behaviors will eliminate defensiveness in your receivers.

_____   8. According to your text, spontaneity can sometimes be used as a strategy.

_____   9. When you truly understand hostile comments, you just naturally accept them.

_____   10.   In order to cope with criticism, you should agree with all the critics' statements.

_____

COMPLETION

The Gibb categories of defensive and supportive behavior are six sets of contrasting styles of verbal and nonverbal behavior. Each set describes a communication style that is likely to arouse defensiveness and a contrasting style that is likely to prevent or reduce it. Fill in the blanks with the Gibb behavior described chosen from the list below.

evaluation   description   control   problem orientation   strategy
spontaneity   neutrality   empathy   superiority   equality
certainty   provisionalism

1.   _____ is the attitude behind messages that dogmatically imply that the speaker's position is correct and that the other person's ideas are not worth considering.

2.   _____ is communication behavior involving messages that describe the speaker's position without evaluating others.

3.   _____ is a supportive style of communication in which the communicators focus on working together to solve their problems instead of trying to impose their own solutions on one another.

4.   _____ is a defense-arousing style of communication in which the sender tries to manipulate or deceive a receiver.

5.   _____ is a supportive style of communication in which the sender expresses a willingness to consider the other person's position.

6.   _____ is a defense-arousing style of communication in which the sender states or implies that the receiver is not worthy of respect.

7.   _____ is a supportive communication behavior in which the sender expresses a message openly and honestly without any attempt to manipulate the receiver.

8.   _____ is a defense-arousing behavior in which the sender expresses indifference toward a receiver.

9.   _____ is a defense-arousing message in which the sender tries to impose some sort of outcome on the receiver.

10. _____ is a type of supportive communication that suggests that the sender regards the receiver as worthy of respect.

11. _____ is a defense-arousing message in which the sender passes some type of judgment on the receiver.

12. _____ is a type of supportive communication in which the sender accepts the other's feelings as valid and avoids sounding indifferent.

MULTIPLE CHOICE

Choose the letter of the defensive or supportive category that is best illustrated by each of the situations below.

a. evaluation   g. description
b. control   h. problem orientation
c. strategy   i. spontaneity
d. neutrality   j. empathy
e. superiority   k. equality
f. certainty   l. provisionalism

_____   1.   Gerry insists he has all the facts and needs to hear no more information.

_____   2.   Richard has a strong opinion but will listen to another position.

_____   3.   Lina kept looking at the clock as she was listening to Nan, so Nan thought Lina didn't consider her comments as very important.

_____   4.   "I know Janice doesn't agree with me," Mary said, "but she knows how strongly I feel about this, and I think she understands my position."

_____   5.   "Even though my professor has a Ph.D.," Rosa pointed out, "she doesn't act like she's the only one who knows something; she is really interested in me as a person."

_____   6.   "When I found out that Bob had tricked me into thinking his proposal was my idea so I'd support it, I was really angry."

_____   7.   "Even though we *all* wait tables here, Evanne thinks she's better than any of us—just look at the way she prances around!"

_____   8.   Clara sincerely and honestly told Georgia about her reservations concerning Georgia's planned party.

_____   9.   The co-workers attempted to find a solution to the scheduling issue that would satisfy both of their needs.

_____   10. "It seems as though my father's favorite phrase is `I know what's best for you' and that really gripes me."

_____   11. "You drink too much."

_____   12. "I was embarrassed when you slurred your speech in front of my boss."

_____   13. "The flowers and presents are just an attempt to get me to go to bed with him."

_____   14. "She looked down her nose at me when I told her I didn't exercise regularly."

_____   15. "Well, if you need more money and I need more help around here, what could we do to make us both happy?"

Choose the letter of the type of coping with criticism that is best illustrated by each of the situations below.

a. ask for specific details of criticism
b. guess about specific details
c. paraphrase to clarify criticism
d. ask what the critic wants
e. ask what else is wrong
f. agree with true facts
g. agree with critic's right to perceive differently
    h. ask about the consequences

Criticism: "You never seem to care about much."

_____   16. "Are you referring to my not going to the office party?"

_____ 17. "You're right that I didn't call you back within 24 hours."

_____ 18. "What do you want me to care more about?"

_____ 19. "I can see why you'd be upset with me for not coming to the party because you've told me you want me to be more involved with your work's social events."

_____ 20. "When I didn't come to the party, were you embarrassed or something?"

_____ 21. "So not calling you back right away was a problem. Have I upset you any other way?"

_____ 22. "So you're upset that I'm not visiting you every week, and you think that shows a lack of affection on my part—is that it?"

_____ 23. "What do you mean?"

_____ 24. "You're correct in that I couldn't visit this week because of finals."

_____ 25. "Because I wasn't at the party, it reflected badly on you?"

Identify which element of a clear message is being used in each statement according to the following key:

a. behavioral description
b. interpretation
c. feeling
d. consequence
e. intention

_____ 26. That's a good idea.

_____ 27. I'm worried about this course.

_____ 28. Jim looked angry today.

_____ 29. I want to talk to you about the $20 you borrowed.

_____ 30. I notice that you haven't been smiling much lately.

_____ 31. I don't know whether you're serious or not.

_____ 32. I'm glad you invited me.

_____ 33. Ever since then I've found myself avoiding you.

_____ 34. I'm sorry you didn't like my work.

_____ 35. I want you to know how important this is to me.

_____ 36. It looks to me like you meant to embarrass me.

_____ 37. After the party at Art's, you seemed to withdraw.

_____ 38. I see you're wearing my ring again.

_____ 39. From now on you can count on me.

_____ 40. I've never heard you say a curse word before.

_____ 41. . . . and since then I've been sleeping at my dad's house.

_____ 42. Because that occurred, they won't work overtime.

_____ 43. Dith sighed and looked out the window.

_____ 44. I'm excited about the possibility.

_____ 45. I'll get another place to live.

STUDY GUIDE ANSWERS

CROSSWORD PUZZLE

The crossword answers (reading across and down):

- 1 Down: displacement
- 2 Across: controlling
- 3 Down: dissonance
- 4 Across: ambiguous
- 4 Down: apathy
- 5 Down: interruption
- 6 Across: confirming / 6 Down: cononant
- 7 Down: co
- 8 Across: compensation / 8 Down: ce / complain
- 9 Down: imperve / impervious
- 10 Across: disconfirming
- 11 Across: climate
- 12 Across: intention
- 13 Across: impersonal

TRUE/FALSE

1. T	3. F	5. F	7. F	9. F
2. F	4. T	6. T	8. T	10. F

COMPLETION

1. certainty
2. description
3. problem orientation
4. strategy
5. provisionalism
6. superiority
7. spontaneity
8. neutrality
9. control
10. equality
11. evaluation
12. empathy

MULTIPLE CHOICE

1. f	10. b	19. g	28. b	37. b
2. l	11. a	20. b	29. e	38. a
3. d	12. g	21. e	30. a	39. e
4. j	13. c	22. c	31. b	40. a
5. k	14. e	23. a	32. c	41. d
6. c	15. h	24. f	33. d	42. d
7. e	16. b	25. b	34. c	43. a
8. I	17. f	26. b	35. e	44. c
9. h	18. d	27. c	36. b	45. e

CHAPTER ELEVEN

Managing Interpersonal Conflicts

OUTLINE

Use this outline to take notes as you read the chapter in the text and/or as your instructor lectures in class.

I. **THE NATURE OF CONFLICT**
    A. **Conflict Defined**
        1. Expressed struggle
        2. Perceived incompatible goals
        3. Perceived scarce resources
        4. Interdependence
        5. Interference from the other party
    B. **Conflict Is Natural**
    C. **Conflict Can Be Beneficial**

II. **CONFLICT STYLES**
    A. **Avoiding (Lose-lose)**

    B. **Accommodating (Lose-Win)**
    C. **Competing (Win-Lose may degenerate to Lose-Lose)**
        1. Passive-Aggression
        2. Direct Aggression
    D. **Compromising (Partial Lose-Lose)**
    E. **Collaorating (Win-Win)**
    F. **Which Style to Use?**
        1. Relationship
        2. Situation
        2. Other person
        3. Your goals

III. **CONFLICT IN RELATIONAL SYSTEMS**
A. **Complementary, Symmetrical, and Parallel Styles**
        1. Complementary
        2. Symmetrical
        3. Parallel

B. **Intimate and Aggressive Styles**
        1. Nonintimate-Aggressive
        2. Nonintimate-Nonaggressive

    3. Intimate-Aggressive
    4. Intimate –Nonaggressive
    5. Traditionals, separates and intimates
    6. No single best style

C. Conflict Rituals
    1. patterns of behavior
    2. problematic if the *only* pattern

IV. VARIABLES IN CONFLICT STYLES
A. Gender
    1. Socialization
    2. Situation

B. Culture
    1. Individualism versus collectivism
    2. Low-context versus high-context
    3. Indirect and direct
    4. Ethnicity
    5. Biology and environment

V. CONSTRUCTIVE CONFLICT SKILLS
A.   Identify Your Problem and Unmet Needs
    1. Who owns the problem?
    2. Identify relational needs

B. Make a Date

C. Describe Your Problem and Needs
    1. Clear messages
    2. Listening and paraphrasing

D. Consider Your Partner's Point of View

E. Negotiate a Solution
    1. Identify and define the conflict
    2. Generate a number of possible solutions
    3. Evaluate the alternative solutions
    4. Decide on the best solution

F. Follow Up the Solution

VI. CONSTRUCTIVE CONFLICT: QUESTIONS AND ANSWERS
A. Isn't Win–Win Too Good to Be True?
B. Isn't Win–Win Too Elaborate?
C. Isn't Win–Win Negotiating *Too* Rational?
D. Is It Possible to Change Others?

KEY TERMS

accommodating
avoiding
collaborating
competing
complementary conflict style
compromising
conflict
conflict ritual
crazymaking
direct aggression
lose-lose problem solving
parallel conflict style
passive aggression
relational conflict style
symmetrical conflict style
win-lose problem solving
win-win problem solving

ACTIVITIES

11.1 UNDERSTANDING CONFLICT STYLES

Activity Type: Skill Builder

PURPOSE

To understand the styles with which conflicts can be handled.

INSTRUCTIONS

1. For each of the conflicts described below, write responses illustrating the five types of conflict styles.
2. Describe the probable consequences of each style.

1. Your dad wants and expects you to spend every Thanksgiving with his whole extended family. You and some close friends who don't have large families want to get away for those four days and do something different. Your dad already arranged your transportation home.

    Avoiding (Lose-lose) response _____

    _____

    Probable consequences _____

    _____

    Accommodating (Lose-Win) response _____

    _____

    Probable consequences _____

    _____

    Competing response _____

    _____

    Probable consequences _____

    _____

    Compromising (Partial Lose-Lose) _____

    _____

    Probable consequences _____

    _____

    Collaborating (Win-Win) _____

_____

Probable consequences _____

_____

2. A fan behind you at a ballgame toots a loud air horn every time the home team makes any progress. The noise is spoiling your enjoyment of the game.
   Avoiding (Lose-lose) response _____

_____

Probable consequences _____

_____

Accommodating (Lose-Win) response _____

_____

Probable consequences _____

_____

Competing response _____

_____

Probable consequences _____

_____

Compromising (Partial Lose-Lose) _____

_____

Probable consequences _____

_____

Collaborating (Win-Win) _____

_____

Probable consequences _____

_____

3. Earlier in the day you asked your roommate to stop by the store and pick up snacks for a party you are both hosting this evening. Your roommate arrives home without the food.
   Avoiding (Lose-lose) response _____

_____

Probable consequences _____

_____

Accommodating (Lose-Win) response _____

_____

Probable consequences _____

_____

Competing response _____

_____

Probable consequences _____

_____

Compromising (Partial Lose-Lose) _____

_____

Probable consequences _____

_____

Collaborating (Win-Win) _____

_____

Probable consequences _____

_____

4. You and Marc share a cubicle and a computer at work and you are both responsible for the same
    amount and type of work. Marc arrives a few minutes earlier than you and stays on the computer
    for several hours, then begins his non-computer work. You would be able to work more efficiently
    if you had some time on the computer early in the day.
    Avoiding (Lose-lose) response _____

_____

    Probable consequences _____

_____

    Accommodating (Lose-Win) response _____

_____

    Probable consequences _____

_____

Competing response _____

_____

Probable consequences _____

_____

Compromising (Partial Lose-Lose) _____

_____

Probable consequences _____

_____

Collaborating (Win-Win) _____

_____

Probable consequences _____

_____

5. You and your spouse have to make a decision about your 5-year old's schooling. You believe strongly in supporting public schools and having children attend the neighborhood school. Your husband believes he didn't get a good education in public school and since you can afford to, you should send your child to private school.
    Avoiding (Lose-lose) response _____

_____

Probable consequences _____

_____

Accommodating (Lose-Win) response _____

_____

Probable consequences _____

_____

Competing response _____

_____

Probable consequences _____

_____

Class_____   Name _____

Compromising (Partial Lose-Lose) _____

_____

Probable consequences _____

_____

Collaborating (Win-Win) _____

_____

Probable consequences _____

_____

_____

What styles are easiest to use with family? With friends? At work? With strangers? Why?

_____

_____

_____

_____

_____

11.2 YOUR CONFLICT STYLES

Activity Type: Invitation to Insight

PURPOSE

To identify the styles you use to handle conflicts.

INSTRUCTIONS

1. Use the form below to record three conflicts that occur in your life that you are comfortable analyzing.
2. For each, describe your behavior, show how it fits the definition of conflict, classify your conflict style, and describe the consequences of your behaviors.
3. Summarize your findings in the space provided.

INCIDENT	YOUR BEHAVIOR	HOW IT MEETS THE DEFINITION OF CONFLICT. Expressed struggle Perceived compatible goals Perceived scarce resources Interdependence Interference of other party	YOUR CONFLICT STYLE Avoid Accommodate Compete Compromise Collaborate	CONSEQUENCES
EXAMPLE *My friend accused me of being too negative about the possibility of finding rewarding, well-paying work.*	*I became defensive and angrily denied his claim. In turn I accused him of being too critical.*	*This was clearly an expressed struggle and I perceived interference in my choice of jobs. Possibly we both perceived scarcity of the reward of feeling good about ourselves.*	*Competing*	*After arguing for some time, we left each other, both feeling upset. I'm sure we'll both feel awkward around each other for a while.*
1.				

242

INCIDENT	YOUR BEHAVIOR	HOW IT MEETS THE DEFINITION OF CONFLICT. Expressed struggle Perceived compatible goals Perceived scarce resources Interdependence Interference of other party	YOUR CONFLICT STYLE Avoid Accommodate Compete Compromise Collaborate	CONSEQUENCES
2.				
3.				

CONCLUSIONS

1. Are there any individuals or issues that repeatedly arouse conflicts?

_____

_____

2. What conflict style(s) do you most commonly use? Do you use different styles with different people or in

   different situations? Why or why not?

   _____

_____

_____

_____

_____

Class_____   Name _____

3. You can go online to http://jeffcoweb.jeffco.k12.co.us/high/wotc/confli1.htm and take a brief quiz about your approaches to conflict (are you a turtle, shark, bear, fox, or owl?). How do these animals compare to the labels used in the text?

_____

_____

4. Choose one or more of the conflicts you described in which you did not use a collaborative style and explain how you could have used a collaborative style. Predict what would have happened.

_____

_____

_____

_____

_____

5. Are you satisfied with your usual way(s) of approaching conflict? Why or why not?

_____

_____

_____

Adjust the number of lines so this fits on one page. _____

11.3 THE END VS. THE MEANS

Activity Type: Invitation to Insight

PURPOSE

To distinguish the ends from the means in a personal conflict.

INSTRUCTIONS

1. In each of the conflict situations below, identify the <u>ends</u> each party seems to be seeking. There may be ends that the relationship shares as well as individual ends for each of the parties involved.   Ends in a conflict are the overall, general (often relational) goals that the dyad has.
2. Brainstorm a series of possible <u>means</u> that could achieve each person's (and the relationship's) ends. Means are the many possible ways to reach the end state.
3. Record conflict situations of your own, identifying ends and means.

CONFLICT SITUATION	SHARED ENDS	SPEAKER'S ENDS	OTHER'S ENDS	POSSIBLE MEANS
EXAMPLE *My friend wants me to visit her in Washington and meet her family. I'd like to visit, but it would cost a lot, and I'd rather save the money for something else.*	*We both want to maintain the affection in the relationship. We both want one another to know we are important to one another and that we care about one another and our families.*	*I want to spend as little money as possible while still letting my friend know how important she is to me. I don't want to lose her friendship.*	*She wants to show her family what a good friend I am and have some companionship while she has to stay in Washington.*	*She/her family sends me money to go to Washington. We share the cost. I combine whatever else I want to do with a short trip to Washington. We arrange for the family to meet me when they next come to our city. My friend comes back with her sister or mother to spend time with me.*
1. My roommate wants a friend (whom I dislike) to sublease a room in our apartment.				
2. I'm dating a person who's of a different race than I am, and my family thinks this is a mistake.				

CONFLICT SITUATION	SHARED ENDS	SPEAKER'S ENDS	OTHER'S ENDS	POSSIBLE MEANS
3. My older sister thinks that I'll turn into an alcoholic when I have a few beers (there are a few alcohol problems in our family). I tell her not to worry, but she won't get off my case.				
4. My mom keeps asking me about my grades and nagging me on the issue of my boyfriend. She thinks I'm going to make the same mistakes as she did.				
5. Some people in my office listen to country music all day. I've got nothing against it, but it gets old. I'd like more variety.				
6. Your example:				

11.4 WIN–WIN PROBLEM SOLVING

Activity Type: Invitation to Insight

PURPOSE

To help you apply the win–win problem-solving method to a personal conflict.

INSTRUCTIONS

1. Follow the instructions below as a guide to dealing with an interpersonal conflict facing you now.
2. After completing the win-win steps, record your conclusions in the space provided.

Step 1: Identify your unmet needs (i.e., the situation, the person(s) involved, the history, etc.).

_____

_____

Step 2: Make a date. (Choose a time and place that will make it easiest for both parties to work constructively on the issue.)

_____

Step 3: Describe your problem and needs (behavior, interpretation, feeling, consequence, intention) Avoid proposing specific means or solutions at this point.

_____

_____

_____

_____

Step 3A: Ask your partner to show that s/he understandings you (paraphrase or perception-check).

_____

_____

Step 3B: Solicit your partner's point of view/clear message (behavior, interpretation, feeling, consequence, intention).

_____

_____

_____

_____

Step 4: Clarify your partner's point of view (paraphrase or perception-check as necessary).

_____

_____

Step 5: Negotiate a solution.

   a. Restate the needs of both parties (what both have in common).

      _____

      _____

   b. Work together to generate a number of possible solutions that might satisfy these needs. Don't criticize any suggestions here!

      _____

      _____

      _____

      _____

      _____

   c. Evaluate the solutions you just listed, considering the advantages and problems of each. If you think of any new solutions, record them above.

      _____

      _____

      _____

   d. Decide on the best solution, listing it here.

      _____

Step 6: Follow up the solution. Set a trial period, and then plan to meet with your partner and see if your agreement is satisfying both your needs. If not, return to step 3 and use this procedure to refine your solution.

_____

_____

Class_____   Name _____

CONCLUSIONS

In what ways is this procedure similar to or different from the way in which you usually deal with interpersonal conflicts?

_____

_____

_____

Was the outcome of your problem-solving session different from what it might have been if you had communicated in your usual style? How?

_____

_____

_____

_____

In what ways can you use the no-lose methods in your interpersonal conflicts? With whom? On what issues? What kinds of behavior will be especially important?

_____

_____

_____

_____

What concerns or hesitations do you have about using the win-win approach? Why?

_____

_____

_____

_____

Class_____   Name _____

11.5 CONFLICT RESOLUTION DYADS
Activity Type: Oral Skill

PURPOSE
To develop your skills in using the win–win conflict resolution methods introduced in Chapter 11 of *Looking Out/Looking In.*

INSTRUCTIONS
1. Join with a partner and discuss conflicts from your lives. Choose one that would be suitable for a win-win conflict attempt. One of you will role-play a real life partner.
2. Engage in the win–win conflict resolution methods introduced in Chapter 10 of *Looking Out/Looking In.* (You may use 11.4 to help you prepare this conflict.)
3. Use the *Checklist* below to evaluate your performance (or videotape the conflict dyad and evaluate one another's performance).
4. On a separate sheet of paper, evaluate your performance in this dyad, and describe how this method can be effectively and realistically applied to everyday conflicts.

Set a "date" for discussing the issue   _____

Describes unmet needs to partner   _____
— other's behavior
— your interpretations
— your feelings
— consequences (for self and/or other)
— intentions

Seeks verification that partner understands statement of needs   _____

Solicits partner's needs, as appropriate   _____

Actively listens/perception checks to verify understanding of partner's needs   _____

Negotiates win–win solution to best possible extent   _____
— identifies/summarizes conflict
— generates possible solutions without criticizing
— evaluates alternatives
— decides on win–win solution

Plans follow-up meeting to modify solution as necessary.   _____

Describes how this method can be applied to everyday conflicts   _____

TOTAL   _____

11.6 MEDIATED MESSAGES – CONFLICT MANAGEMENT
Activity Type: Group Discussion

PURPOSE

To manage conflict in mediated contexts.

INSTRUCTIONS

Discuss each of the questions below in your group. Prepare written answers for your instructor, or be prepared to contribute to a large group discussion, comparing your experiences with those of others in your class.

1. In your experience, does conflict occur more rapidly or less rapidly in mediated contexts (e.g. e-mail, instant messaging/chat, telephone).

_____

_____

_____

2. Describe how mediated communication channels might help or hinder the brainstorming process (an important aspect of win-win problem-solving). Would the level of emotion involved make a difference? Why or why not?

_____

_____

_____

3. Describe gender and/or cultural differences in conflict management that might occur in mediated contexts.

_____

_____

_____

4. Describe whether in your experience certain mediated contexts tend to promote the use of particular conflict styles and whether or not conflict is easier or harder to manage using particular mediated channels.

_____

_____

_____

11.7 YOUR CALL – CONFLICT MANAGEMENT

Activity Type: Group Discussion

PURPOSE

To apply conflict management principles to a relationship.

INSTRUCTIONS

Use the case below and the discussion questions that follow to discuss the variety of communication issues involved in effective communication. Make notes on this page, add other pages on your own, or prepare a group report/analysis based on your discussion. Add your own experiences to individualize the analysis to make it **Your Call**.

CASE

Klaus and Drew have been roommates for two years, and they have had very few problems. But this term Klaus has a difficult and early class schedule, and he has taken on more hours at work to make ends meet. Drew's parents support him completely and he has a very light schedule this term. Klaus and Drew's friends continue to come to their house to party, and Drew is very irritated with Klaus because he's always studying and is a big bore all of a sudden. Klaus thinks Drew is a spoiled brat and insensitive to his needs. Neither Klaus nor Drew has said anything at this point.

1. Should Klaus and Drew bring this conflict out in the open? Would airing their differences be beneficial or harmful to the relationship?

   _____

   _____

   _____

2. What are the unmet needs of Klaus and Drew in this situation? Should they keep those unmet needs to themselves and use an avoidance style or should they use one of the other personal conflict styles?

   _____

   _____

   _____

3. Evaluate the potential of the win-win problem-solving method to solve this situation.

   _____

   _____

   _____

STUDY GUIDE

CHECK YOUR UNDERSTANDING

CROSSWORD PUZZLE

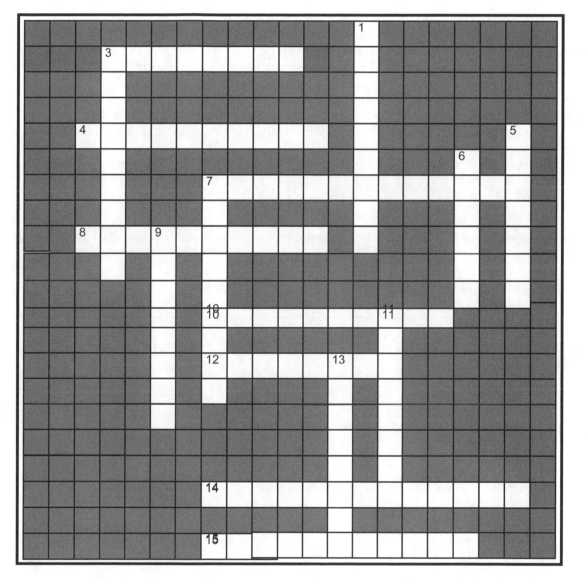

DESIGNER: TAKE OUT THE FIRST 3 AND LAST SPACE OF 2 ACROSS. THE # 3 IS NOW USED FOR BOTH DOWN AND ACROSS

ACROSS

3. ignoring or walking away from conflict
4. When two or more people are in a long-term relationship they develop their own _____ conflict style, a pattern of managing disagreements over time.

7. a nonassertive response style in which the communicator submits to a situation rather than attempt to have his or her needs met
8. an approach to conflict resolution in which both parties attain at least part of what they wanted but neither's needs are totally met
10. intense arguing and caring deeply about each other is an intimate-_____ style
12. an expressed struggle between at least two interdependent parties who perceive incompatible goals, scarce resources, and interference
14. a relational conflict style in which partners use different but mutually reinforcing behaviors
15. a relational conflict style in which both partners use the same tactics

DOWN

1. an approach to conflict resolution in which neither side achieves its goals
3. a direct expression of the sender's needs, thoughts, or feelings, delivered in a way that does not attack the receiver's dignity (a clear message is an example of this)
5. an approach to conflict resolution in which the parties work together to satisfy all their goals
6. an unacknowledged repeating pattern of interlocking behavior used by participants in a conflict
7. a style in which the person is unwilling to confront a situation in which his or her needs are not being met
9. a relational conflict style in which the approach of the partners varies from one situation to another
11. _____-nonagressive relationships don't have much attacking or blaming and do manage to keep conflict issues from interfering with their relationship.
13. communication that is an oblique way of expressing wants or needs in order to save face for the recipient

TRUE/FALSE

Mark the statements below as true or false. Correct statements that are false on the lines below to create a true statement.

_____   1. Gender and culture rarely have an impact on the types and styles of conflict.

_____   2. Conflict will occur only if there is not enough of something (money, love, respect, time, etc.) to go around.

_____   3. Very close and compatible relationships will not involve conflict.

_____   4. Effective communication during conflicts can actually keep good relationships strong.

_____   5. Avoiding is always a bad idea.

_____   6. Passive aggressive styles can be seen as a type of competing.

_____   7. Competing is clearly superior to other conflict styles to get what you want.

_____

_____   8. Crazymaking is just another name for passive aggression.

_____

_____   9. "It takes two to tango"—in conflict, as in dancing, men and women behave in totally similar ways.

_____

_____   10. The first step in win-win problem solving is to make a follow-up plan.

_____

COMPLETION

Fill in the blanks with the crazymaker term described below. If you need help, see page 375 in *Looking Out, Looking In.*

avoiders	pseudoaccomodators	guiltmakers	subject changers	distracters
mind readers	trivial tyranizers	gunnysackers	beltliners	trappers

1. _____ don't respond immediately when they get angry. Instead, they let conflicts build up until they all pour out at once.

2. _____ do things they know will irritate their conflict partner rather than honestly sharing their resentments.

3. _____ engage in character analyses, explaining what the other person *really* means, instead of allowing their partners to express feelings honestly.

4. _____ set up a desired behavior for their partners and then when the behavior is met, they attack the very thing they requested.

5. _____ refuse to fight by leaving, falling asleep, or pretending to be busy.

6. _____ try to make their partners feel responsible for causing their pain even though they won't come right out and say what they feel or want.

7. _____ refuse to face up to a conflict either by giving in or by pretending that there's nothing at all wrong.

8. _____ use intimate knowledge of their partners to get them "where it hurts."

9. _____ attack other parts of their partner's life rather than express their feelings about the object of their dissatisfaction.

10. _____ escape facing up to aggression by shifting the conversation whenever it approaches an area of conflict.

MULTIPLE CHOICE

Match the terms below with their definitions.

_____   1. win-lose

_____   2. indirect communication

_____   3. "Vesuvius"

_____   4. conflict style

_____   5. passive aggression

a. an indirect expression of aggression, delivered in a way that allows the sender to maintain a façade of kindness
b. an oblique way of expressing wants or needs in order to save face for the recipient
c. an uncontrolled, spontaneous explosion involved in conflict
d. an approach to conflict resolution in which one party reaches its goal at the expense of the other
e. a pattern of managing disagreements that repeats itself over time in a relationship

Choose the letter of the personal conflict style that is best illustrated by the behavior found below.

a. avoidance
b. accommodation
c. compete/direct aggression
d. compete/passive aggression
e. compromise
   f. collaborate/win-win

_____   6. Stan keeps joking around to keep us from talking about commitment.

_____   7. "I can't believe you were so stupid as to have deleted the report."

_____   8. Even though he wanted to go to the party, Allen stayed home with Sara rather than hear her complain.

_____   9. Alternating bicycling and using a car, roommates are able to share expenses for only one car.

_____   10. A smoker and nonsmoker agree that smoking on the balcony meets both their needs.

_____   11. Rather than tell Nick about his frustration over Nick's not meeting the deadline, Howard complained to others about Nick's unreliability while maintaining a smiling front to Nick.

_____   12. Carol wouldn't answer the phone after their disagreement because she was afraid it would be Nancy on the other end.

_____   13. Seeing John's obvious distress, Terrell put aside his work to listen to John for a half-hour. This didn't totally meet either's needs, but did partially meet each person's needs.

_____   14. Even though Sage could see Kham's distress, she told him she had a deadline to meet in one hour and asked if they could talk then.

_____   15. (Sarcastically) "Oh, sure, I *loved* having dinner with your parents instead of going to the party Saturday night."

Choose the best answer for each statement below.

16. When partners use different but mutually reinforcing behaviors, they illustrate a

   a. complementary conflict style
   b. symmetrical conflict style
   c. parallel conflict style
   d. supportive conflict style

17. When both partners in a conflict use the same kinds of conflict behaviors, we say they have a _____ conflict style.

   a. complementary
   b. symmetrical
   c. parallel
   d. supportive

18. Partners who fight but are unsuccessful at satisfying important content and relational goals have a _____ style.

   a. intimate-aggressive
   b. intimate-nonaggressive
   c. nonintimate-nonaggressive
   d. nonintimate-aggressive

19. Partners who avoid conflicts—and one another—instead of facing issues head-on have a _____ style.

   a. intimate-aggressive
   b. intimate-nonaggressive
   c. nonintimate-nonaggressive
   d. nonintimate-aggressive

20. Partners who have a low amount of attacking or blaming, who confront one another either directly or indirectly, but manage to prevent issues from interfering with their relationship have a _____ style.

   a. intimate-aggressive
   b. intimate-nonaggressive
   c. nonintimate-nonaggressive
   d. nonintimate-aggressive

CHAPTER 11 STUDY GUIDE ANSWERS

CROSSWORD PUZZLE

Crossword answers:

Across:
3. avoiding
4. relational
7. accommodation
8. compromise
10. aggression
12. conflict
14. complementary
15. symmetrical

Down:
1. lose-lose
3. assertion
5. win-win
6. ritual
9. paradigm
10. avoidance
11. intimate
13. indirect

TRUE/FALSE

1. F	3. F	5. F	7. F	9. F
2. F	4. T	6. T	8. T	10. F

COMPLETION

1. gunnysackers
2. trivial tyranizers
3. mind readers
4. trappers

5. avoiders
6. guiltmakers
7. pseudoaccomodators
8. beltliners

9. distractors
10. subject changers

MULTIPLE CHOICE

1. d	5. a	9. f	13. e	17. b
2. b	6. a	10. f	14. f	18. d
3. c	7. d	11. d	15. c	19. c
4. e	8. b	12. a	16. a	20. b